TECHNICAL EDUCATION:

WHAT IT IS,

AND WHAT AMERICAN PUBLIC SCHOOLS SHOULD TEACH.

AN ESSAY

BASED ON AN EXAMINATION OF THE METHODS AND RESULTS OF TECHNICAL EDUCATION IN EUROPE, AS SHOWN BY OFFICIAL REPORTS.

By CHARLES B. STETSON.

BOSTON:
JAMES R. OSGOOD AND COMPANY,
(LATE TICKNOR & FIELDS, AND FIELDS, OSGOOD, & CO.)
1874.

BOSTON:
STEREOTYPED AND PRINTED BY RAND, AVERY, & CO.

CONTENTS.

TECHNICAL EDUCATION.

CHAPTER I.

INTRODUCTION.

THE education required by a people is not a fixed quantity. That which is adequate for one generation or for one locality is not, necessarily, adequate for another generation or for another locality. It may be said, in general, that the education of a people should always conform to their necessities; that, as the conditions of life change, the education of a people should undergo a corresponding change: it may be one of degree or of character, or it may be a change involving both. The present is a time when those who have the shaping of popular education in America should consider anew the practical application of this simple truth.

For the American laborer, whether in the work-shop, in the counting-house, or on the farm, the conditions of life have, within the last fifty years, undergone a radical change, and of such a nature, that the laborer must now receive a vastly better education than he required one or two generations ago: otherwise he cannot advance himself as he should, nor even maintain his old position. This will be evident from a simple glance at three or four things which strikingly distinguish his present situation from his past.

Competition no longer Local, but World-wide. — First, the railroad, steamship, and telegraph have changed, in a marked degree, the condition of the American laborer. Before they came, the competition he had to meet was almost wholly local. If he did his work as well and as cheaply as those who went to the same church, or sat on the same jury, with himself, there was for him no need of further concern. He, and these neighbors of his, fixed the price of their products, since they sold in a market from which all but local competition was virtually excluded. There is nothing of this now. Telegraphy and steam have made, as it were, one neighborhood of the whole world; and the competition the American laborer must now meet, even at his own door, is no longer local: it comes from the ends of the earth. In a market admitting the competition of the world, those who go to the same church, or sit on the same jury, cannot longer determine the price of their products. The world, of which they are but a part, settles that.

Has an Ohio farmer a fleece of wool to sell? He meets in the market the wool-grower of Australia. Has a Minnesota farmer a bushel of wheat to dispose of? The return for it depends, more or less, on the crop in California, or along the shores of the Black Sea. Is the seller a cotton-manufacturer of Lowell? He must compete with the looms of Lancashire. A Maine manufacturer of axes? He must face the axe-maker of Birmingham, whom he has, by the way, driven from the American market, while he successfully competes with him in the market of the world. Is it a Philadelphia builder of locomotives? He feels the influence of Creuzot, though he may never have actually met a French locomotive on this side of the Atlantic. Is it an American ship-builder? He knows, to his sorrow, that there are other builders on the Clyde. Indeed, there is scarcely one product of American industry, whose market-price is not now determined, in large degree, by the competition of the whole world; and this as the result, mainly, of steam-carriage and telegraphic communication. The more efficient these new instrumentalities become, the sharper will be the world's competition, reaching even the most secluded hamlet.

The destiny of the laborer is, perhaps, more influenced by steam as a carrier than by steam as a producer; for steam, especially when aided by telegraphic communication, is a great leveller in the world of industry. No levelling produces just the same pleasing effect for all. Take England as an illustration. Having established her manufactures when her insular position and sail-carriage gave her comparatively easy access to the European and other markets, she now finds herself everywhere confronted by products which the railway has brought from the manufacturing centres of interior Europe. While she glories in the railway achievements of her Stephenson, those very achievements have greatly diminished the vantage which was previously hers in the market of the world. But what of vantage she has lost through steam and telegraphy, she is now struggling to recover through a better education of her producing classes. By the same levelling process the American laborer is affected. Unless he does his best, he is liable to be driven from the market, even of his own town, by a producer who lives hundreds, perhaps thousands, of miles away.

Here, then, is one particular in which the life of the American laborer has undergone a decided change; for him competition is no longer local, but world-wide.

LAND ONCE NEW AND FERTILE, NOW OLD AND IMPOVERISHED. — Consider, in the next place, the land. When it was new, bone and muscle, vigorously exercised, were enough to insure an abundant harvest. Whatever was planted grew without stint; nor were there a thousand pests to destroy the fruits of the earth. The American farmer, then, had little occasion for chemistry, geology, botany, entomology, engineering, to secure immediate and satisfactory results. As the remote result, however, of the stupid agriculture of the past, the present generation inherits vast tracts of impoverished, unproductive soil. It may be found everywhere, from the Atlantic seaboard to the Mississippi, from the Lakes to the Gulf. But little of the land which has been cultivated for two generations, now yields as well as it did forty years ago. Much of it, indeed, is returning to a state of nature.

The work of exhaustion still goes on. What is to check it? for it must be checked. What is to restore the land already impoverished? for it must be restored. No American farmer should consent to go into the market with wheat, corn, butter, cheese, mutton, beef, cotton, which have cost him more than the same things have cost his competitors. But he must do this, unless he puts into his work something more than bone and muscle, something more than the equally stupid energy of reapers and steam-ploughs. There must be labor, indeed, but no wasted labor. That there may be no waste, the labor must always harmonize with the invisible forces of Nature, — those sleepless, ever-active giants with whom it is easy to work, against whom it is impossible for the farmer to achieve any thing. It is educated mind, working through bone and muscle and machinery, which is to restore the impoverished lands, and keep them at their highest point of profitable production, whatever that may be. In England that point is, for wheat, about twenty-seven bushels to the acre.

Here, then, is a second particular — diminished productiveness of much of the soil — in which a decided change has come over the life of many American laborers.

MANUFACTURES NO LONGER FEW AND RUDE. — In the third place, the demands upon the American artisan have increased wonderfully. Fifty years ago it was a very limited variety of products required at his hands: to-day the variety is almost infinite, ranging from a tenpenny nail to an ocean steamship; from a pair of spectacles to a telescope for exploring the most distant nebulæ. But the change is not indicated alone by a wonderful increase in the variety of the manufactures. Raw material and bone and muscle constitute a much smaller part of their value; while skill and taste count for vastly more than they did when the shoemaker boarded around as well as the schoolmaster, and made the shoes and boots for the neighborhood. The house, and the furniture put into it, must have more of elegance and comfort. The fabrics of the loom must be more beautiful in design, and must show a higher finish, than in the days of homespun. More graceful forms must issue from the founderies, glass-works, potteries, and quarries. The ship must have a better model; and its workmanship must be finer in every part. Indeed, though the work of the American artisan is, as a whole, far behind that of some other portions of the world, yet there has been decided progress not only in the variety, but in the quality, of the products.

The progress in taste is largely attributable to the importation of foreign designs and designers. It may, however, be said generally, that the progress in American manufactures is due to individual effort and to the subdivision of labor. There has certainly been no united, systematic effort to produce skilled workmen, except so far as the literary education of the public schools has indirectly contributed to such a result. This indirect contribution has not been a slight one, however. The subdivision of labor has enabled the workman to learn one part of his business more thoroughly by remaining ignorant of all the other parts. He has thus become a more dexterous workman in a limited field, but not, necessarily, a more skilful workman; that is, he knows no more, necessarily, but less, perhaps, about the underlying principles of his business, than he did when he served an apprenticeship, and got some knowledge of all parts of his business.

It is essential, then, that the American artisan receive a much better technical education than present opportunities permit. It is essential for him, individually, that he may hold his own with his fellows; it is essential for the capitalist who employs him, that he may hold his own in the market of the world: and so it is essential for the common welfare. It is only the skilled labor of the multitude which will suffice. It is not enough that there be a few men highly qualified for their work; it is not enough that there be intelligent direction; it is not enough that the artist work under the same roof with the artisan: director, artist, and artisan should be, as far as possible, united in the same person. The less the artisan resembles a machine, the better and cheaper will be the products of his labor. All this will be placed beyond question by the unimpeachable evidence which will be given in subsequent pages. It will be seen that it is not the pauper labor, but the educated labor, of Europe, like that seen in

Creuzot, France, which America has good reason to fear. It will be seen that the cheapest of all labor is skilled labor, such as every State may secure by properly educating her citizens.

Here, then, is a third particular — multiplied and improved manufactures — in which a decided change has come over the life of a large class of American laborers.

Decay of Apprenticeship. — In the fourth place, apprenticeship has become almost wholly a thing of the past in America, and largely so in Europe. Yet there never was a more urgent demand for skilled workmen.

This decay of apprenticeship is mainly due to the subdivision of labor which is now observed in the manufacture of nearly all things, from pins to locomotives, because it is found to yield the best results. The use of machinery, the character of which is often such as to put an end to small enterprises, has promoted this subdivision by accumulating workmen in large groups. The beginner, confining himself to one department, is soon able to earn wages. This gratifies both himself and his parents; and so he usually continues as he began. If, however, he wishes to become a master of his trade, and the employer agrees to instruct thoroughly, the latter is often tempted to keep his apprentice at work an undue time in the department he may have first well learned, and in which his labor is, consequently, profitable. If the employer does not yield to this temptation, then who is there to give the apprentice proper instruction, seeing that so many workmen usually work by the piece, and cannot afford to spend any time in the instruction of others? Nobody. Thus it happens that the beginner usually confines himself to one department, and is only anxious to receive wages as soon as possible.

While this is to the present advantage of employer and employed, it is to the ultimate disadvantage of both; for it is found that the workman who knows all the departments of his trade — knows the theory as well as the practice — will always do better work in any particular department he may devote himself to. Again: the workman who can do but one thing, or rather one part of one thing, has little chance for promotion. He also finds himself helpless, when, at some unfortunate turn, his limited specialty fails him; and there is more frequently an excess of workmen in a subdivision of any industry than an excess in the industry as a whole. Furthermore, the use of machinery, instead of diminishing, rather increases, the artisan's need of thoroughly understanding his trade: unless he does, he cannot make the most of about the only chance (an increase of daily wages) which he now has for bettering his condition. Machinery having rendered individual enterprises so expensive, the artisan has, in most cases, little chance of ever becoming his own master. Twenty-five years ago, when there were, for example, more daily papers in Boston than now, and more shoe-manufacturing employers in New England, the industrious, frugal artisan working for wages had a reasonable hope that he might some day become an employer himself. That hope, as a stimulating, lifting power, must have been wonderfully productive of good. But what, in any department of industry, is there now to lift the workman, to stimulate him to greater exertion? Virtually, nothing but a prospective increase of his *per diem* by doing more and better work, and by a merited promotion to some one of the many subordinate places of oversight and trust. He should, therefore, be provided with every means for improving himself as a workman, and qualifying himself for promotion. Apprenticeship having essentially departed never to return in its ancient form, something else must take its place in America, as its place has already been largely taken in Europe by special schools, and give the American artisan that technical instruction which he must have, or perish.

Here, then, is a fourth particular — the decay of apprenticeship — in which a decided change has come over the life of a large class of American laborers.

LABOR, RUDE, DEXTEROUS, SKILLED. — It is thus

seen, from the four particulars enumerated, that the times have decidedly changed for the American laborer; that it is now of the utmost moment for him, whatever his work, to be skilled in the full sense of the word; and that he cannot become thus skilled without instruction having such an object in view. But what is skilled labor and its value?

All manual labor may be divided into rude, dexterous, and skilled labor. The first requires only, or mainly, the strength and patience of the stupid plodder. The second requires nice finish, and celerity of execution: but the work is all done by "rule of thumb;" that is, in ignorance of principles. Subdivision of labor is specially favorable to the production of dexterous workmen. The third requires both dexterity, and a knowledge of underlying principles. It is theory and practice united; and it enables the workman to adapt himself to new conditions, and always to do the best thing in an emergency, — to improve old methods of work, or devise new ones. It may be said, in general, that, while the rude laborer earns one dollar, the dexterous laborer will earn two dollars, the skilled laborer three dollars; all working with their hands. In some varieties of labor, the difference is much greater than this.

For the rude laborer there is no hope of promotion; for the merely dexterous laborer the prospect is limited:

but the skilled laborer, master of his business in theory and practice, may count surely upon advancement. In dull times the skilled laborer is the last to be discharged; yet he is the one who has savings to rely upon, — the one who can most readily adapt himself to a new occupation.

There are but few kinds of labor, giving employment to comparatively few persons, which require only the rude strength of the steady plodder. Such stupid drudgery is the exception; while labor requiring a greater or less degree of skill is the law. Frequently, indeed, labor is degraded to drudgery by reason of the stupidity with which it is performed. It may, therefore, be justly said, that almost every laborer should possess skill; the more skill the better. Even in sawing wood, spading earth, tending a cotton-picker, there is a philosophy, a best way to proceed, which the intelligent, but not the stupid, laborer is sure to discover and to follow.

Popular Education. — But there can be no such general diffusion of skill among laborers, without a popular education beginning in the primary school, and having that for one of its objects. Hence it is quite time American schools, instead of longer proceeding much as they did forty years ago, recognized the change in the social situation; quite time they were so modified as, by direct intention, to educate the pupils more for skilled laborers, — farmers, artisans, merchants, manufacturers — than for the literary and professional occupations. When the best possible result of this kind has been secured, there will always be inevitable blockheads enough to do the inevitable drudgery of the world. They who oppose the systematic technical education of workmen, fearful that there will then be none left ignorant enough for drudges, need not be alarmed. Nor will a little early industrial culture be wasted, even on those who may become theologians or judges; but rather it will do them good.

But how should the popular education be modified? To-day it may be described as literary, — for the use of the head, and not for the use of the hands. Preserving its general character of fifty years ago, it does not bear directly upon the leading pursuits of the people. In the organization of many schools, and in the methods of instruction, there has been great change; but there has been very little change in the things taught, though a large increase in the quantity. The text-books for reading, spelling, arithmetic, grammar, geography, writing, have grown in number and size; and much more time is devoted to each of these studies. Indeed, in nearly all the public schools of the land they occupy five-sixths of the pupil's time. Could the school-year be doubled in length, twice as much time as now would be given to the studies enumerated, if the educational spirit of the past, which is, in the main, the American educational spirit of the present, continued to control the schools, as it does now control them with few exceptions. It would be more arithmetic, more geography, more grammar, more spelling, with no fundamental change of character.

There is, however, a growing tendency to modify American popular education, and to bring it into harmony with the age and the manifest demands of labor. What has already been well done in some parts of Europe, and what the other parts (notably England, so thoroughly alarmed by the International Exhibitions, beginning with the one in London in 1852) are making such zealous efforts to do, will doubtless soon be regarded by all Americans as, in the main, the proper thing for the technical education of American labor. It is with this technical education that European governments are just now specially concerning themselves; and it is with the same thing that they who have the shaping of popular education in America must specially concern themselves during the next twenty-five years. In the present public-school system, with its strong literary features, they have a broad and excellent foundation upon which to build. No amount of instruction in science and art can fully compensate for lack of literary training, even when industrial results alone are sought.

Natural Science a Part of Popular Education. — This harmony between education and the demands of the age requires that the natural sciences, — like chemistry, botany, physiology, — which bear directly upon great industries, and otherwise tend to promote the common welfare, should form a distinguishing feature in popular education, — should be added to the present literary curriculum of the American public school. The whole people should not only be made acquainted with the leading principles and the more important practical applications of natural science, but they should be so instructed as to acquire, in good degree, the scientific habit of investigation and thought. The farmer has daily need of this knowledge in the performance of his routine labors; also daily need of this habit of investigation and thought in order to meet emergencies, — to meet the cases not laid down in the books, nor inherited through tradition. Lacking this knowledge and this habit of mind, he wastes his energies in a blind contest with the invisible forces of nature, and draws the most absurd conclusions, or no conclusions at all, from surrounding phenomena. For him labor degenerates into drudgery; while profits diminish, or disappear altogether. Then there are many artisans who have urgent need of similar knowledge, and of a similar habit of mind. By the same things the kitchen, too, would be greatly profited; cost of living would be reduced, yet people would fare better, and their years would be prolonged.

While, as it will be claimed, it is not the business of the common school to make specialists, — farmers, carpenters, accountants, engineers, cooks, — it is the business of such a school to teach at least the elements of technical knowledge, and to teach these elements to all. Such instruction, because of the discipline it affords, — like in part, in part unlike, that afforded by other studies, — is of indirect value to every one. It is also of direct value to the great body of the people; for it is the universal European experience, that laborers cannot be satisfactorily educated for their work, unless they have first received, in schools for children and youth, not only literary instruction, but also instruction in the elements of technical knowledge, scientific and artistic. With a broad foundation of elementary instruction, and not otherwise, special instruction can be successfully added according to the requirements of each workman. Such is the universal experience of those European countries that have undertaken to educate workmen for their special pursuits.

Drawing a Part of Popular Education.—This harmony between education and the demands of the age also requires that drawing should hold a conspicuous place in popular education. Both for the peculiar culture it imparts, and for its practical uses, it should be taught in every public school. As the result of extended and careful investigations, made from time to time, for the purpose of determining the character of the education requisite to produce skilled workmen and promote industrial welfare, European governments now lay greater emphasis upon drawing than upon any other study. Indeed, it holds so prominent a place in the education of the people of most European communities, that it may be said, roundly, to constitute a fourth part of all the education the artisan receives. And yet even in France, where the artisan has for some time been well educated in drawing, it is regarded of vital importance that the present instruction in drawing be increased, and made of still better quality. Indeed, the evidence places it beyond question, that, in Europe, the welfare of the individual artisan, of manufacturing establishments, of whole communities even, may be justly attributed to instruction in drawing. As drawing has no particular home, it may render to American industry services equally valuable. The whole people should not only be made acquainted with its leading principles and more important industrial applications; they should be so instructed as to acquire, in good degree, artistic habits of mind and manipulation.

Almost every thing that is well made now is made from a drawing. In the construction of buildings, ships, machinery, bridges, fortifications, nothing is done without drawings. It is not enough that there be draughtsmen to make the drawings: the workmen who are to construct the objects required should be able, without help, to interpret the drawings given for their guidance. This they cannot do without instruction that acquaints them with the principles on which the drawings are made, and so trains the imagination as to enable it to form from the given lines a vivid mental picture of the object required. The workman who lacks this knowledge and this ability, as it is probable that nineteen-twentieths of American artisans now do, must work under the constant supervision of another, doing less and inferior work, and receiving inferior wages. But it is also essential that the workman himself be able to make at least a rude working-drawing, whenever, as frequently happens, an emergency requires it.

Furthermore, it is not enough that the artisan be able to make an object, and to make it expeditiously; not enough that his workmanship be of the highest order. There are thousands of things whose commercial value depends mainly upon their beauty, for which the world is always so willing to pay. This beauty may be in the form of the objects themselves, or in the applied decoration, or in both. However strong a piece of carpeting may be made, however exquisite may be its finish, an ugly design will ruin its sale. It is the design, no less than the quality of the workmanship, that determines whether or not an object from the furniture factory, from the glassworks, or the pottery, shall sell for more than the cost of the raw material. It is the same with Nature's products. The beautiful horse is preferred to the one equally serviceable, but homely. Indeed, beauty has a commercial value almost unlimited. But wherever the beauty is found, — in the shape of the object or in the decoration, — it is mainly due to form; and so its principles and their applications are best learned by persistent practice in drawing.

It is not enough, however, that there be special designers. In most departments of industry, the workmen who are to reproduce given designs in the form of commercial products cannot do this successfully, unless they have received such a training as to give them an artistic taste and the power of artistic manipulation. This training they must have, if they are simply to reproduce given designs; but they also need it, that they may be able themselves to modify the given design (as it is often necessary to do), the better to adapt it to the object required, or to the material of which it is made. The evidence, indeed, leaves it in no doubt that the artisan should receive an artistic training (the more of it the better), of which drawing should constitute the chief element. The best results have been secured, where the one who designed and the one who executed were the same person; the next best results, where the one who executed had received an artistic training. It may be accepted as a general truth, the more of an artist, the better the artisan; for the work will ever tell of the workman. Hence it is of the utmost importance that instruction in drawing should go far beyond exercises in mere copying; that the principles of good design should be thoroughly taught; and that the pupils, from an early age, should be systematically trained in the pleasant and intellectually stimulating production of original designs.

How Time is to be had for the New Studies. — The two great features which should be ingrafted on popular education in the United States, if that education is to be brought into harmony with the times and the manifest requirements of labor, have now been designated. They are practical science and practical art.

But how can these additions be made? Whence

is the time to be had for the instruction of the boys and girls in the public schools, most of whom fail to accomplish all that is now required of them? Yet there is no study now in these schools which should be excluded. The evidence is incontrovertibly strong, that the best technical education alone is not sufficient to produce even the best practical results: there must also be literary culture, the more of it the better. Never was there a broader and firmer foundation upon which to build a popular industrial education than is afforded by the public schools of the United States. This foundation must be preserved, and, if possible, made better still. But how can new studies be added, and new and old receive proper attention?

When the necessity of adding new studies is fully recognized, a way will be found. Doubtless it will be found, upon considering just how much of each study it is essential to teach, — that some, if not all, of the present studies can be greatly abridged without diminishing the quality of the mental discipline acquired, or the amount of really useful knowledge. Would the spelling-books, for example, be of less service, were the words they contain reduced to one-third of their present number, and confined to those in common use? This reduction would save the pupils many days which they now devote to the task of spelling words they will never have occasion to spell when they are once out of school. Would the instruction in geography be of less value, if it were limited to the general principles and to the more important facts; which the pupils would be able to retain after they were once learned? This would reduce by two-thirds those details which are now memorized only to be forgotten; and the pupils would save months of time. And would it not be better to confine arithmetical instruction to the science of numbers and its practical applications? Doubtless it will also be found that some of the schools, if not all, can be made much more efficient by change in their organization or methods of instruction. Why, for example, should the bright, healthy, industrious pupils in graded schools be required to go the same pace as the stupid and lazy? Why, indeed, may there not be such a flexible school organization as to afford each a chance to do his best, — to finish any study at the earliest moment? Why not reduce the lessons in arithmetic, geography, grammar, to four a week, and even drop these studies an occasional term? Thus would time be secured for new studies without increasing the daily lessons of the pupil. And doubtless it will be found that parents, when they realize the great value of instruction in practical science and practical art, will send their children to school longer than most of them do now. As for suitable teachers, they will be had as they are wanted. But, after the present public schools have done all it is proper for them to undertake, much additional technical instruction must be provided for American workmen in special schools, as is now the case in so many parts of the civilized world. These special schools, except the higher ones, must be adapted to the requirements of the different localities where they are established. In one place the school must be, in the main, commercial; in another place, agricultural; and, in a third place, it must be adapted to those engaged in building, in wood, leather, or textile manufactures, in quarrying, in locomotive or machine construction, or whatever else may be the chief pursuit.

Object of this Compilation. — It is the object of these pages, mainly filled with extracts from governmental reports, to give a general idea of what has been done for the technical education of workmen in Europe, how it has been done, what the evident results are, and what it is there urged should be further attempted. As the testimony is foreign, it is of special value for Americans, since it shows them the character of the competition they must meet in the market of the world. It is hoped, therefore, that this, though slight, contribution in favor of a modified education for the American people will not be wholly without influence with those who have the special care and moulding of the public schools of the country. It is hoped that it will strengthen and somewhat accelerate the general movement now beginning in behalf of popular industrial education. Much precious time has already been irretrievably lost; and, for a generation to come, American laborers must feel the evil consequences. In a matter which depends upon the education of the whole people, there must always be patient waiting for results. Nothing can be achieved at a bound.

While so little has been done for industrial education in America, so much has been done, and is now doing, in other countries, that it must be many years, even with the best possible effort, before American farmers, manufacturers, and artisans, as a body, can equal the skill of many of their foreign competitors. Because the fullest results cannot be immediately secured, that is no argument for further neglecting the industrial education of the people, but rather an argument for the speediest and most vigorous action in its favor. Though we stand still, other nations will not. But it is not simply a matter of foreign competition: there is the home competition of State with State, of city with city, of one establishment with another, and of one artisan or farmer with another. No tariff can protect any community against this home competition.

Where manufactures are already established, they can

be permanently retained only by the technical education of the workmen in local schools. Though these manufactures have hitherto been successful in spite of unskilled labor, it will be hazardous in the extreme to rely upon such labor hereafter, or upon skilled labor to be got by chance from abroad. Where it is the wish to establish new manufactures, there the manufactures, if they are to be made secure and profitable, must be established on the technical education of the workmen in local schools. That is the only foundation upon which it is safe to build the new, or to which it is safe to trust the old, unless the manufactures are very rude indeed, and owe their value mainly to the raw material consumed.

The Manufactures of most Value. — But the manufactures for which a community should specially contend are those in which skilled labor counts for much, and raw material for very little. As such manufactures require a good degree of intelligence for their successful prosecution, they yield the largest profits, and afford the best class of citizens. That is not all. The demand for the products of skilled, artistic labor, is not limited by the number of purchasers, but only by their taste, and by their desire and ability to purchase. The demand is, therefore, essentially unlimited. Thus a shawl costing five hundred dollars because of its beauty will always be preferred to another equally warm and durable, but costing only ten dollars. On the other hand, the demand for simple, rude manufactures,—like ploughs, carts, shovels, hammers, jeans, plain cottons, which only require to be well fitted for use, and substantially made,—is limited by the number of purchasers, who take the least possible amount, and of the cheapest variety, that will serve their turn. It is much the same with these manufactures as it is with the staple products of agriculture, the demand for which is limited by the number of the consumers rather than by their ability to purchase; since the rich man can consume no more bread than the poor man, while the latter must have as much as the former for his healthy, vigorous support.

The labor-saving implements now employed in American agriculture, enabling one man and two horses to cultivate each year forty to sixty acres of land on a Western prairie, does not increase the products of the earth beyond the fixed amount required by the population, but reduces the number of laborers engaged in agriculture. Whatever facilitates the cultivation of the soil inevitably tends to diminish the relative number of farm-laborers, and to increase the relative number of those engaged in other pursuits. It is to the use of labor-saving implements on the farm that is to be largely attributed the greater relative growth of American cities compared with the increase of the agricultural population. In Europe, a similar relative increase in the city population over that of the country is largely due to a more intelligent cultivation of the soil, whereby the same labor obtains much larger returns than it formerly did; and so there is a demand for less farm laborers compared with the whole population. When a high degree of skill is added to the labor-saving machinery now employed in American agriculture, there will be seen a yet greater relative increase of the city and manufacturing over the agricultural population.

This increasing multitude of artisans will not be able to find profitable employment as rude workmen. There is a rigid limit fixed to the demand for rude products, as already indicated. They will be able to find profitable employment only as skilled, artistic workmen, — employment in the production of all those things which skill and taste know so well how to create for the embellishment and delight of civilized life, and for which there can be no rigidly limited, but always an increasing demand. It is for such manufactures that communities should specially contend, and, to contend successfully, must educate their people in practical science and in practical art. When a military result is required, the whole people must be educated in the military art, as Prussia has demonstrated by putting the spiked helmet into all of her schools. When an industrial result is required, then the whole people must be educated in the industrial arts, as Switzerland has exemplified so well. The earliest day is the best day to begin this work of education. Those communities which first establish their manufactures have a decided initial advantage over all new competitors, though not a sufficient advantage to justify them in neglecting any precaution against encroachment. Since, then, skilled labor is the only sure foundation for prosperous manufactures, and since the artisan class is increasing, and must, for the reasons given, continue to increase, in relative numbers and importance, much more rapidly than the whole population, the proper education of this class becomes, with each succeeding year, a matter of more vital consequence.

The following pages will clearly show that the technical education of workmen cannot be made in the highest degree efficient, unless it begins in the primary school; and that instruction in art and science alone is not enough, but must be based on general literary culture. The American system of common schools already gives every one the general culture, to which those fundamental elements of technical education which belong alike to nearly all departments of labor can be easily added without making specialists of the pupils. After the common school must come the special schools, even now so numerous in Europe. The following pages will also clearly show that drawing and art must occupy the most conspicuous place in the technical education of workmen. They will also show that different European governments have been, for a series of years, making earnest, systematic efforts — and perhaps nothing so engrosses their attention now — for the technical education of workmen; beginning it in primary schools, and continuing it through evening schools, Sunday schools, apprentice schools, schools of arts and trades, popular lectures and museums, with its culmination in great technical universities. To-day it is with educated, skilled labor — ever the cheapest as it is the best labor — that Europe proposes to meet the world in friendly contest for industrial supremacy. Let America take note that it is the educated, skilled labor of Europe, and not pauper labor, as so many believe, which she has good reason to fear, and against which she can defend herself only by educating her workmen equally well.

CHAPTER II.

VALUE OF TECHNICAL INSTRUCTION.

THE numerous extracts given in this chapter show clearly, among other things, that,

1. The person who has general charge of any business should understand that business both theoretically and practically. His knowledge of principles should be such as to enable him to instruct any subordinate requiring instruction, to determine at once the comparative value of different processes of work, or to invent new ones when emergencies require it. In a word, he should be able to reach just conclusions at once by his knowledge of principles, and not slowly by "trial and error." He should be workman enough to know when work is well done, that he may not be cheated by those under him, and that he may be able to render justice unto all by duly discriminating between the skilled and the unskilled laborer. He should understand his business as a whole, and the relation of each part to the

whole. Neither skilled workmen nor tariffs can compensate for stupidity on the part of the superintendent. Only the very few exceptional geniuses, like Stephenson, become thus qualified to take charge of enterprises, great or small, without special school instruction.

2. The workman should not only be dexterous in manipulation; he should certainly know so much of the theory of his business as will enable him readily to comprehend all instructions, verbal or graphic, given for his guidance. The more extended and thorough his knowledge of principles, the better. Such a workman requires very little supervision: he executes with rapidity; he wastes the least possible; he adapts himself readily to new methods; he devises novel and better ways for doing even the simplest things; he is the first to be promoted; he is the last to be discharged; he always commands the best wages, and yet his labor is the cheapest in the market. On the other hand, the workman who works only by "rule of thumb," though he may be dexterous, lacks logic, lacks invention, lacks adaptability; indeed, is only a better kind of machine.

3. The workman should be better instructed because of the machinery used; since it is the rude or dexterous workman, rather than the really skilled workman, who is supplanted by machinery. Skilled labor requires thinking; but a machine never thinks, never

judges, never discriminates. Objects which have a simple and regular form, and require high finish, or not, may be made with advantage by machinery, if the objects are produced in large numbers. Most kinds of work which demand little besides strength for their execution can usually be best done by machinery too. Though the employment of machinery does, indeed, enable rude laborers to do many things now, which formerly could be done only by dexterous workmen, yet, after making allowance for all the bearings of the question, it is clear that the use of machinery has decidedly increased the relative demand for skilled labor as compared with unskilled labor; and there is abundant room for an additional increase, if it is true, as declared by the most eminent authority, that the power now expended can be readily made to yield three or four times its present results, and ultimately ten or twenty times, when masters and workmen can be had with sufficient intelligence and skill for the direction and manipulation of the tools and machinery that would be invented.

4. All those persons whose business it is to produce new combinations of matter — such as the farmer, miner, dyer, bleacher, founder, maker of machinery, and numerous others — should have a knowledge of chemistry. Without such knowledge, which is an

essential element of skilled labor in these departments of industry, neither rude nor dexterous labor can produce satisfactory results.

5. The utmost effort should be made to produce articles of beautiful design, whether in form, or in color, or both. The difference between good design and poor design is the difference between success and failure in the market of the world. When the beauty of the object depends, as it usually does, upon its own form, or upon the form of the applied decoration, the workman should be one who has been thoroughly instructed in artistic drawing and designing. Not only should the originator of the design have been thus instructed, but also the reproducer of the design in wood, metal, earth, or other substance.

6. For the most successful prosecution of any great enterprise in land or naval architecture, in the construction of railroads, canals, machinery, there should not only be an abundance of thorough and expert draughtsmen, but each workman should be draughtsman enough to make a drawing of any object he is required to construct. Of two competing establishments, the one having such workmen, the other not, the former would not only win, but would distance the latter every time.

It will be seen that these six points are fully sustained by the testimony of the extracts.

BRITISH OPINIONS EXPRESSED BY CHAMBERS OF COMMERCE.

The Right Hon. Lord Robert Montagu, M.P., Vice-President of the Committee of Council for Education, &c., submitted in 1867, to the Chambers of Commerce in Great Britain, the following questions: —

1. What trades are now being injured by the want of a technical education?

2. How, and in what particulars, are they injured?

3. How do other countries, from their greater attention to technical instruction, absorb our trade? Give instances, and, if possible, statistics.

4. What plan of technical education would remedy the evil?

The replies to these queries as to technical education were ordered by the House of Commons to be printed, March 25, 1868. A summary of the replies will be found in the following: —

Letter from the Chairman of the Association of Chambers of Commerce of the United Kingdom to the Right Hon. Lord Robert Montagu, M.P.

My Lord, — The Association of Chambers of Commerce of the United Kingdom have submitted the questions suggested by your lordship to the respective chambers. It is thought more convenient to give you a summary of the answers, rather than to trouble you with the separate reports, except those from Nottingham, Kendal, the Staffordshire Potteries, and Birmingham; in which the statements are more detailed, and are therefore forwarded with this statement in the same shape as received.

The Birmingham report states, that "every trade in Birmingham and the district is being injured by the want of technical education, and those trades the most in which the cost of the articles produced consists most of labor, and least of the raw material."

The Belfast Chamber reports, that they are not aware of any trade in Belfast and its neighborhood being injured by the want of technical education; but they are convinced that improved education, both technical and general, would indefinitely increase the industrial efficiency of society.

"The higher branches of industrial knowledge, that is to say, mathematics, engineering, and chemistry, both general and as applied to agriculture, are taught in the Belfast Queen's College, in a way that we believe to be most satisfactory. But there is no adequate provision for the instruction in these and similar branches of any class of society below that which sends pupils to the Queen's College."

The Staffordshire Potteries Chamber replies as follows: —

"It would be difficult to say *what* trades are now injured by the want of technical education. The question would, perhaps, have been better put, had it been asked 'What trades *would be* injured, if they could not have imported workmen, or the productions of workmen, who, from having received a better education than the workmen of this country, had thus fitted themselves to perform duties which could not be undertaken by our own people?' If the question be so put, it is only necessary to point out the numerous cases in which foreign workmen are employed, and foreign designs carried out, in most, if not all, of the principal manufactories of this country, — work which might have been performed by English workmen, had they been sufficiently educated for the purpose; the result of which is an increased expenditure to the manufacturers, and, consequently, a greater inability on their part to meet foreign competition, both at home and abroad, resulting in loss to the English workman and the country generally. In the Pottery district, several manufacturers employ foreign workmen as painters and designers; and, in one manufactory, a sum of two thousand pounds a year is paid to foreign workmen."

In reply to the second question, "How, and in what Particulars, are the Trades of this Country injured?" the general purport of the answers is, that among employers, foremen, and workmen, great deficiencies exist in those branches of knowledge which bear most intimately on the great departments of industry. For most trades, a knowledge of design, of theoretical and applied mechanics, and of abstract and applied chemistry, are of the highest importance. The Sheffield Chamber thinks that the steel trade would be benefited, and strengthened against foreign competition, if the foremen were educated in chemistry and metallurgy. The Wakefield Chamber speaks of the "want of theoretical and applied knowledge on the part of the workmen in the various trades in which they are respectively employed, particularly of mechanical drawing as an art, practical geometry required by engineers, cabinet-makers, and mechanics generally, and of chemistry practically applied."

With reference to art, the Nottingham Chamber, while acknowledging the advantages of the present schools of art, states, "that the expense of attending such schools is considered to be too great, and deters the poorer classes from availing themselves of these advantages. It is the opinion of this chamber, that our national system of art-instruction lays too great stress upon high finish in the execution of the work, rather than upon a system of work which would give our art-workmen the facility of rapid and intelligent execution; nor is it successful in training students sufficiently numerous and well educated to take the places now occupied by hundreds of French designers and modellers, and German mechanical draughtsmen. Greater facilities and more encouragement should be given to students of the artisan class; and the present system, however well adapted for teaching drawing, is not favorable to the production of designs with celerity and originality. It is deemed desirable that prizes should be given for sketches and designs drawn within a limited time, and for works from memory."

The answer of the Birmingham Chamber is, that "a large proportion of the multitudinous trades carried on in this district especially suffer, because so many of our manufactured articles are composed of a variety of metals and other materials, which depend for their successful combination and treatment upon a knowledge of chemistry and other sciences, and the beauty of their form on a knowledge of art; while our workmen have scarcely any knowledge of either, but are guided in their work by imitation of one another and tradition."

Referring to the trades of the Kendal district (textile manufactures, dyeing, machine-making, leather, and farming), the report of the Kendal Chamber says, "In these, the workmen, as a rule, are unable to go out of their accustomed groove, and, from want of a knowledge of the scientific principles of their trades, are continually wasting or spoiling material through mistakes which would not occur if they had received a technical education.

"The want of scientific knowledge, and especially of chemistry, is a great obstacle to progress in the manufactures of this district.

The patterns produced by men who have been trained in designing and the principles of color are superior to those produced by the workmen who have not had these advantages. Many manufacturers employing French artists, and others procure their designs from abroad. The trade of pattern-collecting is a recognized one in Paris; and the collector divides his new patterns among his numerous correspondents in England.

"In dyeing, the foreign dyers, especially the French, produce brighter colors than the English; and this is mainly in consequence of the knowledge of chemistry possessed by their workmen. The specimens of manufacture from this locality exhibited last year in Paris excelled in every thing but color.

"The same may be said of the leather trade, in which the best colored leather for fancy purposes is still imported from France; and several of the discoveries for the best treatment of fine leather have been made in France, in consequence of mere knowledge of chemical processes.

"In machine-making, the want of workmen who understand the law, as well as the practice, of mechanics, is severely felt; and this applies to all trades in which machinery is used, especially in the introduction of new machinery.

"In agriculture, a knowledge of chemistry and natural science would be exceedingly beneficial to the farmer; and the need of it is becoming daily more and more apparent. Some of those who have attempted to carry out a little knowledge in the neighborhood have been greatly benefited; and larger and more diffused knowledge would be of incalculable value in developing the productions of the soil."

The Dewsbury Chamber states, that "ofttimes woollen fabrics are spoiled in the dyeing for want of a knowledge of chemistry. Progress in the improvement of the manufacture of textile fabrics is retarded by the want of a more intelligent understanding by the workmen of the various processes; and the duties of workmen in the engineering and machine-making business are imperfectly discharged for want of a better knowledge of the principles of mechanics."*

In reference to the want of mechanical science, the means of instruction are most limited. The Nottingham Report states, that "the machinery, both for the lace and hosiery manufactures of this district, is of an exceedingly ingenious and complex character; but, for want of instruction in mechanical science, the inventive power of the workmen is misdirected, time is lost, many valuable inventions are never perfected, and, if the desired improvements are at last obtained, they are the result, not of scientific induction, but of numerous trials and failures, which a proper technical education would have rendered unnecessary."

The report from the same chamber, referring to the processes of dyeing, states, that "a knowledge of chemistry is essentially necessary for the carrying-on successfully of these trades; but such knowledge does not generally exist amongst either the masters or workmen. Should a master desire to give his son a thorough education in practical chemistry, he must send him to a distance, and incur great expense: whereas his competitors in these arts, both in France and Germany, can obtain the best possible education on the spot, and at a cost of as many shillings as it requires pounds in England. The apprentices and artisans of Chemnitz, which is the great competing town with Nottingham in the hosiery trade, obtain a technical education of the highest class gratis, when it can be shown that they are meritorious, and unable to pay the small fee of the institute. For the same class in Nottingham, there is no instruction that will at all compare with it.

"This chamber has no access to statistics which would show to what extent our manufactures may have been superseded by the manufactures of other countries; but, in many of our articles, we find a growing competition both in our home and foreign markets, owing to the superiority of design and finish of certain classes of goods. In those countries from which we experience the strongest competition, the work-people have the advantage of excellent technical schools, where complete technical education can be obtained at very moderate cost, and in some cases free; and in addition to this, in many parts of the Continent the children of the work-people have all previously received good primary instruction.

"It is shown to this chamber, by the most competent persons, that our workmen, generally, are utterly ignorant of the properties of materials they are daily using, and of the best method of using such materials, and that all attempts at scientific teaching for the working-classes will produce very limited results, as compared with other countries, until a system of primary education, of a more thorough and comprehensive character than that which exists at present, shall have been introduced."

The South of Scotland Chamber (Hawick) states, that "the French are very superior dyers. The manufacturers of Verviers (Belgium) have absorbed a large portion of the woollen-yarn trade of Scotland, by producing a superior article at the price. One of the manufacturers visited Verviers lately, and was informed by one of the most intelligent manufacturers there, that young men who had been at the technical school at Mulheim had made the greatest progress in the business."

The Batley Chamber believes, that "the shawl trade of Leeds has been absorbed by Continental manufacturers by reason of their

4*

technical knowledge, especially as respects the laws of form and color."

Even in processes not connected with textile manufactures, the necessity of improved education is insisted upon by Mr. Freeman (Falmouth Chamber), who writes, —

"My experience here in the management of an extensive business in the granite trade leads me to believe that technical education would be of great advantage to the working-classes and to the trade generally. There has been but little improvement in the character of the tools they use; while at the same time there has been great improvement in the tools used in America, by which a finer finish is given to the work, and labor is much diminished. Without some instruction to make the young mechanic acquainted with the advantages, I see no prospect of inspiring him to the use of them, more especially as the Trades' Union has great power here, and interferes to prevent any alterations in the process of manufacture."

The Newcastle Chamber writes, that although "the want of a technical education amongst the persons employed here has not been generally felt, yet such manufactories as those for engineering, glass, earthen-ware, chemicals, iron, and iron ship-building, and mines for coal, lead, iron, and minerals and clays, would benefit through technical education."

In reply to the third question, "How do other Countries, from their Greater Attention to Technical Education, absorb our Trade?" the answers show that the superior education afforded on the Continent, and which is conducted with special reference to industrial pursuits, enables the manufacturers there to compete with us in departments of industry which hitherto we considered peculiarly our own.

The Macclesfield Report states, "that the silk trade is injured by a superior skill in dye and finish on the Continent, causing a very large increase in foreign competition, which is aided by unequal tariffs and cheap labor abroad."

The Wakefield Chamber replies, "By possessing a thorough theoretical and practical knowledge of their several trades, the designers, dyers, and engineers in foreign countries, produce greater purity and beauty of design, clearer and brighter colors in the cloths and other fabrics they manufacture, finer patterns, and greater lightness, with efficiency combined, in construction, and in a more approved machinery."

The Dewsbury Chamber is of opinion, "that hitherto the heavy woollen trade of this district has not been absorbed, to any great degree, by the woollen manufactories of other countries; but, in lighter and more fancy fabrics (textile), Continental manufacturers supersede us by a greater attention to art-instruction, and the production of good colors in dyeing."

The Kendal Chamber says, "As the trade of the district is principally confined to the United Kingdom, foreign competition is not so severely felt as in some other parts of the country; but there is no reason why, with increased knowledge, several branches of trade that once largely manufactured for exportation should not again return to this neighborhood."

The answer from the Birmingham Chamber is as follows: "In other countries the work-people are instructed in science and art: the effect of this is shown in the rapid improvement of their manufactures, in beauty of form, excellence of finish, adaptation to the purpose for which they are intended, and cheapness; and their excellences enable them now to be in the course of largely supplanting us in the markets of the world."

With reference to the request for statistics, the answer is, that the Government has ample means for ascertaining the great development of trade on the Continent; and to the Birmingham Report will be found appended a list of articles made in Birmingham and the hardware district, which are largely replaced in common markets of the world by the productions of other countries, — a list which might be considerably extended.

With reference to the fourth question, viz., " What Plan of Technical Education would remedy the Evil ? " the answers substantially agree in the following propositions: 1st, THE NECESSITY OF LARGELY INCREASED PRIMARY EDUCATION; 2d, THE ESTABLISHMENT OF SCHOOLS OF SCIENCE AND ART IN THE GREAT CENTRES OF INDUSTRY, AIDED BY GOVERNMENT.

The Kendal Chamber thus states its views: " The advantage which it is sought to obtain by an improved system of technical education is twofold; 1st, It would not only supply the want of such scientific knowledge as bears directly upon the art practised by the workmen; but, 2d, It would overcome that common contractedness of mind which produces an inability to perceive the general purpose of a process apart from its accessories, that inaccuracy in detail which accompanies confusion of thought, and a want of precision in action and the use of terms. Thus it is the habit of mind as well as a deficiency of knowledge which renders it so difficult for the average workman to adapt himself to any improvement, either of process or machinery. This is also the great obstacle to specific scientific instruction.

" It would seem, therefore, that the first object in technical schools should be to train young men to habits of accurate thought, and give them that general enlargement of mind, without which accuracy becomes tyrannical. To this end, the elements of mathematics should be taught and developed, as far as practicable, in an early stage of education.

"Then there is, perhaps, no single acquirement which more expands the mind, 'by showing the possibility of every-day thought,' than gaining a familiarity with a foreign language. For this purpose, the language should be taught by an intelligent, well-educated Englishman, able to develop the structure of his own language, and introduce the elements of comparative grammar.

"Along with this preliminary course of mathematics and language, there should be some instruction in the elements of science, with a view of explaining scientific method, rather than of imparting definite instruction. Then would follow the higher development and teaching of the above, with more detailed and full instruction in those special sciences on which our industries depend.

"But the most prominent object should be, in the technical schools of a high class, thoroughly to instruct the pupils in science proper.

"The question now arises, How this course of instruction is to be given to a large number of young men, without too much interfering with the practical learning of their trades? As some only can give their whole time to study, it is suggested, that, as in many businesses work is not so brisk from December to May as during the rest of the year, it would be possible for many apprentices, or young men learners, to study during five or six winter months without injury to business. Thus they would have six months of practical work alternately with six months at school. By this means they could apply their technical or scientific knowledge, from time to time, more efficiently than they would be able to do by any directly technical instruction given in a continuous course of school education. Besides, coming from the application of acquired knowledge back again to the fount, they perceive the object to be attained by further investigation, and better appreciate what they have to learn by having experienced already how usefully knowledge can be applied.

"It would be a great boon to the poorer students, who would thus provide the expense of half a year's instruction by the labor of the other half, as has often been done by earnest students at the Scotch universities.

"At first, high-class technical schools could only be established in large towns; but by degrees, as the number of competent teachers increased, they should be extended, and schools should be eventually established for the preliminary courses in every town in the kingdom.

"As other associations will deal with the necessity of an infinitely higher class of elementary education being requisite than what is at present taught, should Parliament establish a system of national education, chambers of commerce may limit their observations to a government system applicable to purely technical instruction.

"In France, government aid is given by competitive exhibitions, varying in amount from a fourth of the cost of education to a full payment of the whole of the fees. A similar endowment of merit is attached to technical colleges, where the students are taught, boarded, and clothed. Such a plan enables the cleverest youths in the humbler classes to obtain the best instruction. By means of communal funds, schoolhouses have been erected, and masterships established. The Government has also supplied professors to departmental and local schools.

"If a board of education be established in each county, or division of a county, in England, the best school within its district should have connected with it a technical department. The mode of providing the funds is one for the legislature to settle.

"In districts and towns where the population is engaged in trade, the Government might aid, in terminable loans at a low rate, the erection of school-buildings; attaching to such schools queen's medals and exhibitions for successful students in science and art.

"So stimulated, partly by school-fees and the payment by the employer of the fees of clever youths, together with endowments by liberal and prosperous men of business, technical and scientific schools may be expected to spring up if properly qualified teachers can be found."

The following resolution was passed at a special meeting of the Birmingham Chamber of Commerce, Jan. 10, 1868: —

"That the council be instructed to request the Association of Chambers of Commerce to inform Lord Robert Montagu, M.P., that, in the opinion of this chamber, it is of the utmost importance that government schools of science should be established in the great centres of industry, for the purpose of giving systematic technical education both to the middle and working classes.

"The chamber wish it to be understood, that, by the term 'technical education,' they mean both artistic and scientific instruction."

The Nottingham Chamber is of opinion that the education should be "of a thorough and useful character, and in all cases taught with a view to its application to arts and manufactures. Which of the Continental schools does this most effectually, the Government, with the resources at its command, will ascertain without difficulty. But it is of the highest importance that such institutions should be established immediately, that they should be in no wise inferior to the best Continental schools, and that they should be equally cheap and accessible."

The Batley Chamber recommends, that "a central establishment should be organized and carried on in some town (say Leeds) for this district, and that other places in the district should be affiliated to it on certain conditions. Local classes might be held in the day and night schools, or in mechanics' institutes. We think part of the cost should be paid by Government, and other part by fees from pupils. The direction and supervision of the local classes might (we think) be left to local managers; but we think the central school should be in the hands of some department of Government."

The Hawick Chamber, after making a similar recommendation, adds, "To enable the working-classes to reap the full benefit of the technical schools, a thorough system of national education is required; but there should be no delay in establishing the schools, as there are already numbers of workmen sufficiently well educated to take advantage of them."

The Macclesfield Chamber recommends, "that the present system of primary education should be consolidated, and made compulsory, so as to insure such education being given to every child in the State.

"That local efforts for secondary or technical education should be supplemented by government assistance by way of annual grants, loans," &c.

The Sheffield Chamber recommends the establishment, in that district, of "schools of chemistry and metallurgy in connection with the school of art, but which, if they are to succeed, must not depend for their support on private contributions."

The Wakefield Chamber thinks that the Government ought to establish, in all the great centres of industry in the United Kingdom, schools equal to the best technical schools in France, Switzerland, Prussia, and Saxony.

The Belfast Chamber, on the other hand, states, "We do not see our way as yet to recommend the introduction of any system of 'trade-schools' into Ireland. The subject of technical education is so new to the people of this country, that we cannot feel sure that such schools would be appreciated and supported. What we would suggest as most practicable and desirable is an extension of the course in the national schools, so as to bring instruction in elementary geometry and algebra, mensuration, mechanical and free-hand drawing, and bookkeeping, which branches form the basis of all technical education within the reach of all children, in towns at least, who can give the necessary time."

The Coventry Chamber has passed the following resolution unanimously: "That, in the opinion of this chamber, it is essentially necessary that schools for technical education should be established in the different manufacturing towns; and that the special schools which would be most beneficial to this city and neighborhood comprise those for teaching elementary chemistry, texile manufactures, practical mechanics, and horology."

The Dewsbury Chamber recommends "local schools for the instruction of artisans in the principles of their respective trades,—such schools to be partially supported by local rates, and supplemented by government grants, — together with a central school, to which more advanced students might be sent to receive further education in science and art."

The Staffordshire Potteries Chamber consider that "a plan of education which would remedy this evil would be to establish a system of education in this country, in art and science, which would render it unnecessary for manufacturers to employ foreign talent. This could only be done by a national system of primary and technical education throughout the country, supported, so far as is necessary, from a fund to which all should contribute; for, if the future national prosperity of the manufacturing and trading interests of this country is supposed to depend upon a more efficient system of technical education, the expense of supporting it ought to devolve upon the nation at large, and not, as has hitherto in a great measure been the case, on individuals and localities. Primary education ought to be one of the first considerations, — be made compulsory, as far as possible, with scholarships attached to these schools, so as to enable scholars to obtain by diligence a free education in the higher branches. There can be little doubt that trades' unions have injuriously affected most of the trades of this country; but a good system of education would, in all probability, have a very strong tendency to do away with some of the most objectionable rules at present existing in these unions."

In addition to these evidences of the general feeling among chambers of commerce in all parts of the country in behalf of technical education, the Committee of the Associated Chambers (appointed specially to consider the question) have passed the following resolution: "That, whilst the details of a comprehensive plan of technical education must be the subject of minute examination, the Government be urged to direct its attention at once to the systematic training of professors of theoretical and applied science, and to give increased assistance, beyond that conferred by the late minute on science schools (21st December, 1867), to all serious local efforts to establish and extend the teaching of science and art."

Signed on behalf of the Association,

SAMPSON S. LLOYD, *Chairman.*

Association of Chambers of Commerce of the
United Kingdom, 29 Parliament Street, S.W., Feb. 10, 1868.

Reference is made in the preceding letter to a list of articles furnished by the Birmingham Chamber of Commerce. It is as follows: —

List of some articles made in Birmingham and the hardware district, which are largely replaced in common markets of the world by the productions of other countries. This list might be immensely extended by further investigation, which the shortness of time did not permit.

ARTICLES, OR CLASS OF ARTICLES.	COUNTRIES.
Carpenters' tools; as hammers, pliers, pincers, compasses, hand and bench vices.	Germany, chiefly.
Chains of light descriptions, where the cost is more in labor than in material; as halter-chains and cow-ties, and such like.	Germany.
Fry-pans of fine finish.	France.
Wood-handled spades and shovels, an article of very large consumption.	United States export them to all our colonies.
Hoes for cotton and other purposes, an article of large consumption.	United States compete with us for their own use, and to some extent for export.
Axes for felling trees, &c., an article of large consumption.	United States supply our colonies and the world with best article.
Carpenters' broad-axes, carpenters' and coopers' axes, coopers' tools (various sorts), shoemakers' hammers and tools.	Germany and the United States.
Matchets for cutting sugar-canes, an important article.	Believed to be now Germany.
Nails, cut.	United States export to South America and our colonies.
Nails, wrought.	Belgium.
Nails, point de Paris (wire nails).	French and Belgian largely supersede English.

ARTICLES, OR CLASS OF ARTICLES.	COUNTRIES.
Horse-nails.	Beautifully made by machinery in the United States.
Pumps, of various sorts.	Largely exported by United States. [NOTE. — An American pump found water for the Abyssinian expedition.]
Agricultural implements, — ploughs, cotton-gins, cultivators, kibbling-machines, corn-crushers, churns, rice-hullers, mowing-machines, hay-rakes.	Many articles similar to these are exported by United States to common markets.
Sewing-machines.	United States.
Lamps for use with petroleum, now an article of very large consumption; lamps for the table.	The United-States petroleum lamps supplant the English in India and China; French even imported to England.
Tin-ware, — tinned spoons and cooks' ladles, various culinary articles of fine manufacture and finish.	France.
Locks, — door-locks, chest-locks, drawer-locks, cupboard-locks, in great variety.	United States, France, and Germany.
Door-latches, in great variety.	United States export to Canada.
Curry-combs.	United States and France.
Traps, — rat, beaver, and fox.	United States export to Canada.
Hinges, in wrought iron, for doors, grates, &c., in great variety, gimlets, and augers (twisted).	United States export to Canada, and probably elsewhere.
Brass foundry (cast), as hinges, brass hooks, and casters (great variety), door-buttons, sash-fasteners, and a great variety of other articles.	These articles, in great variety, are now extensively exported from Germany and France.
Brass foundry (stamped), as curtain pins and bands, cornices, gilt beading, and a great variety of other brass foundry.	These articles, in great variety, are now extensively exported from Germany and France.

ARTICLES, OR CLASS OF ARTICLES.	COUNTRIES.
Needles. An article of large consumption.	Mostly from Germany (Rhenish Prussia); even imported to England.
Fish-hooks.	Believed Germany.
Guns. A great variety of sporting guns, articles of large consumption, formerly entirely from Birmingham.	Now exported largely from Liege, Belgium, and St. Etienne, France.
Breech-loading muskets, revolver pistols.	United States.
Watches.	Switzerland and France, even imported into England.
Clocks.	United States and France. [NOTE. — Watches made in United States interchangeable by machinery.]
Iron.	Belgium.
Glass for windows, an article of large consumption, spectacle and all other glasses.	Belgium supplants ours in our own colonies.
Table glass.	Believed to be Belgium and France.
Swords.	Prussia and Belgium.
Jewelry, — gold and gilt, fancy steel; these in very great variety.	France and Germany. These articles are even imported into England.
Small steel trinkets, as bag and purse clasps, steel buttons and chains, key-rings, and other fastenings, and many others in great variety.	France and Germany; many of these even imported into England.
Leather bags, with clasps, purses, &c., courier bags, &c.	Austria, France, and Prussia. We believe about all these articles sold in England are imported.
Buttons, mother-o'-pearl.	Vienna, imported to England.
Buttons, horn.	France, imported to England.
Buttons, porcelain (formerly Minton's of Stoke).	France entirely superseded English, and imported to England largely.
Steel buttons (formerly Bolton and Watts).	France.

ARTICLES, OR CLASS OF ARTICLES.	COUNTRIES.
Florentine or lasting coat-buttons.	Germany.
Steel pens, penholders.	France.
Brass scales and weights.	France.
Cutlery, in great variety, — scissors, light edge tools, such as chisels, &c.	Germany.
Pins for piano-strings, and other small fittings for pianos.	France.
Silver wire for binding the bass strings of pianos, &c.	France.
Iron gas-tubing.	Germany.
Elastic bells, with metal fastenings.	Germany.
Brass chandeliers and gas-fittings.	Prussia and France.
Harness buckles and furniture.	Prussia and France.
German silver, — spoons, forks, &c.	France, Austria, and Prussia.
Locks, — best trunk - locks, best door and cabinet locks.	Prussia and France.
Umbrella furniture.	France and Prussia
Horn combs.	Prussia.
Pearl and tortoise-shell articles.	France and Austria.
Iron wire.	Prussia and Belgium.
Iron and brass hooks and eyes.	Prussia and France.
Bronzed articles.	Prussia and France.
Hollow-wares, enamelled.	Prussia and France.
Optical instruments.	France, Austria, and Bavaria.
Mathematical instruments.	France, Austria, and Bavaria.
Japanned wares.	Germany and France.
Bits and stirrups.	Belgium and France.
Coach-springs and axle-trees.	France.
Electro-plated wares, customers preferring French goods.	France
Gas-fittings.	United States.
Weighing-machines.	United States.
Plumbers' brass foundry.	United States.
Table glass ware.	United States.
Doors, locks.	United States.
Machines for domestic purposes, as sausage-machines, coffee-mills, and washing-machines.	United States.

ARTICLES, OR CLASS OF ARTICLES.	COUNTRIES.
Nuts and bolts.	United States.
Penknives and scissors.	United States.
Stamped brass-ware (certain kinds).	United States.
American "notions," as buckets, clothes-pegs, washing-machines, agricultural machines.	United States.

THE WORSTED TRADE OF BRADFORD.

The following letter from Mr. Jacob Behrens to Lord Robert Montagu, Vice-President of the Committee of Council on Education, England, gives an interesting account of the worsted trade of Bradford. The great success of the past is largely due to a limited amount of technical instruction, which must be hereafter increased, or Bradford will lose her pre-eminence.

BRADFORD, Jan. 24, 1868.

MY LORD, — By a circular which the Secretary of the Association of Chambers of Commerce has addressed to the various chambers, it was intimated that you desire to receive answers to the following four questions : —

1st, What trades are now injured by the want of technical education ?

2d, How, and in what particular, are they injured ?

3d, How do other countries, from their greater attention to technical education, absorb our trades ? Give instances, and, if possible, statistics.

4th, What plan of technical education would remedy the evil ?

As a member of the Committee on Technical Education which was appointed by the Associated Chambers in November last, I had to consider these four important questions; but, having long taken an active interest in all matters relating to education, I venture to trouble your lordship with my own personal views, without in any way prejudging the answer which the Committee will, no doubt, be prepared to return.

In discussing these questions from an essentially local point of view, I shall be able to enter into details which cannot be included in an answer from a body representing all the trades and industries in the United Kingdom.

I also suppose, that, in addressing all the chambers of commerce, it was desired to elicit information with reference to the local want of technical education at the principal seats of trade, which, when collected, may enable the Council for Education to obtain a general view of the wants of the whole country.

Before answering the four questions, I must beg permission to suggest that a great service would be rendered to the public by the statement of the exact meaning which the council attach to the words "technical education."

In the absence of any such precise definition, almost every discussion upon this subject (and hardly a day passes without it being referred to in public) degenerates into a discussion on education in general.

Your lordship will perceive that I have used the term in a wider sense than as the merely practical and theoretical teaching of mechanical and chemical science.

In answer to the first two questions, I may state that the principal industry of this town and district is the manufacture of worsted goods, and that perhaps in no other trade has the absence of scientific instruction been less injurious to a more rapid development.

Nor can we complain of that trade being materially injured by the want of technical education; for the worsted trade of this neighborhood is yet the largest in the world, and has been estimated to amount to thirty-three million six hundred thousand pounds in 1864.

Notwithstanding this satisfactory condition of our trade, signs are not wanting, and they are perfectly palpable to every one engaged in the export trade, that other countries are endeavoring keenly to dispute our pre-eminence.

If we have attained our present position in spite of a deficient state of theoretical instruction (and I believe in no other great seat of industry have there been fewer schools of science than in this part of Yorkshire), the practical education as given in our factories must have been extremely good.

We must, however, remember, that, until lately, we had great and exceptional facilities for the worsted trade; which, by degrees, became concentrated in the immediate neighborhood of Bradford and Halifax.

The population of this district has for centuries been trained in the combing, spinning, weaving, and dyeing of the long wool grown in this and some neighboring counties, and nowhere out of England.

Machine-combing, the power-loom, and the invention in dyeing, hereinafter referred to, gave an immense impetus to our trade; and thus Bradford, which in 1831 had only 43,527 inhabitants, numbered 106,218 in 1861; and 130,000 is a moderate computation for the present.

Our being first in the field gave us many advantages, and we have thus not felt the pressure of foreign competition so soon as some other industries; but, notwithstanding the superiority which we still claim, we are conscious that we cannot afford to go on in the old way much longer.

We not only export the machinery which enables our competitors abroad to comb, spin, and weave in the same manner that we do; but our superior workmen accompany these machines to teach foreigners how to use them.

Our operative dyers, although, as a rule, ignorant of the first principles of chemistry, have invented a very ingenious process by which vegetable and animal fibres can be dyed together, and have become so skilful in this branch of their trade, that our black and color dyers find employment at high wages all over the continent of Europe.

The machines we export are, in many cases, worked by persons possessing a superior education, and, consequently, a more developed intellect than our ordinary mill-hands; and, above all, the owners and managers of many foreign factories apply the results of their scientific training to our machines, and improve them to a degree which already compels us to acknowledge a marked superiority in some of their productions.

Foreign dyers, possessing a thorough knowledge of chemistry, have brought the finish of worsted goods to a perfection which we do not equal; and foreign pattern-designers, who appear to possess a more cultivated taste than ours, show by their productions that they know how to apply it for the benefit of their employers.

Special instances of superior foreign workmanship are not uncommon, but each may be the result of various causes; and it is perhaps impossible in any one case to ascribe it to the superior technical education of our competitors alone.

But, whatever may be the cause, competition on the part of foreign countries has become a serious fact, which deserves our most earnest consideration.

The mills at Rheims produce, from Australian wools, merinos, the perfection of which we have never been able to approach.

The worsted mills at Notts, in Belgium, employ the same kind of weft and warp as we do, but weave fancy goods which are preferred to ours in neutral markets, such as Switzerland and others.

Germany, and principally Saxony, import annually above five million pounds' worth of our worsted yarns; of which a great part is re-exported to the United States, manufactured into fancy goods.

Thousands of pieces of Orleans (cotton and worsted woven together) are every year sent to France to be dyed and finished there, which would not be done if the French had not improved upon the original invention of our operative dyers.

It is perfectly true that in some, even in most instances, the superiority of foreign produce may consist merely in a more careful attention to what we are here too much in the habit of considering small matters. Sometimes it is the finish, or a closer study of each country's peculiar taste or special requirements; but, in the aggregate, the results are important enough to obtain in many cases the preference in neutral markets for the goods which have had the benefit of such attention or such study.

It may therefore be reasonably assumed that the owners of these establishments, having derived their practical instruction from us, were frequently able to improve upon our practice by their having had the further benefit of a superior system of primary and secondary education, and by taking advantage of the many means that are offered to them for the acquirement of technical and scientific knowledge.

The ready access to museums and art galleries, with which many of them are privileged, affords facilities for educating and cultivating their taste, which must also be a great advantage to them.

It is perfectly clear, that we shall have to adopt similar means of improvement if we wish to maintain and improve our position; but, unfortunately, we do not at present possess the appliances for education which alone can make commerce and industry a liberal profession.

Our local teaching of science is so imperfect, that our master-dyers, who require to introduce a more scientific element into their establishments, cannot find amongst their men, and amongst the youths in the neighborhood, the acquaintance with the principles of chemistry and physical science which is necessary for the delicate adjustment of the chemical agents they have to deal with.

Not confining my definition of technical education to mechanics and chemistry, but including in it the training for commercial pursuits, I may state that the ignorance of modern languages, of the geography and the laws and customs of foreign nations, which is yet prevalent amongst the rising generation, even of the affluent classes, is a great bar to their commercial progress, and has been one great means of throwing almost the whole of our Continental export trade into the hands of foreigners residing in this town.

We feel that a better preparation for the trade or industry in which we are engaged would enable us to meet foreign competition with a better chance of success, and that the absence of such training must be injurious to the best interests of England.

Our young men who are to become the future masters of the large factories erected by their fathers, even those who have had the questionable advantage of a so-called first-rate *commercial education*, require, in addition, a thorough scientific training to enable them to meet on equal terms the young men of the same class abroad.

They leave school early, and are taught in their father's mill the father's trade, in the same practical manner in which he himself has learned it, and which has enabled him to rise to his present position, when England possessed exceptional advantages over all other countries.

It is now generally admitted that something more is required, if the young men of the rising generation are to maintain the position created for them by their fathers.

The answers given to the first two questions apply also to the third; but I may mention that the trade of Bradford is not "absorbed" by any other place or country.

We may have abandoned the manufacture of some articles for which other places appear to have superior natural or social facilities; but we have created other branches, which, in ordinary times, give more than sufficient employment to a rapidly increasing population.

We feel nevertheless, and very keenly, that, even in the production of articles in which we excel, we begin to be very hardly pressed by other countries, which, until lately, were very far behind us, — particularly by Germany, Belgium, and France.

When we examine into the causes of their success, we find that they all have one advantage which we do not possess; namely, a better system of technical education.

Considering, also, that fifty years of peace, and the application of steam as a motive-power and to locomotion, have in a great measure deprived England of the exceptional privileges which she possessed formerly in her accumulated wealth and in her geographical position, we are naturally anxious that others shall not outstrip us in the race by means of superior training.

Although the same kind of loom will work equally well in England as in Saxony, there will be a great difference, whether the overlooker who superintends its working, and even the weaver who attends upon it, are intelligently trained workmen, or mere automata.

The man who understands the construction not only of this particular loom, but that of all other looms, must be a more efficient overlooker, or manager, than the mere mechanic of our factories.

I have already referred to the disadvantages connected with the merely practical training of our dyers, and to the necessity for their obtaining a scientific knowledge of their trade.

The German clerk — who has a good knowledge of three or four languages, who has been taught to understand the working of the exchanges in the whole world, the tariffs of different countries, and their commercial laws and usages — will find employment, and rise into an important position or to independence, much sooner than the English clerk, who has not received the same educational advantages.

We expect a remedy for all these evils from the movement which is now making such auspicious progress; and it may not be out of place to mention the fact, that an attempt to impart technical instruction has been signall successful in Bradford.

Years ago it was felt that some artistic education had become necessary, if we wished to retain even a portion of our fancy trade.

Schools of design and a school of art were established; and, though not numerously attended, they were very useful by giving to our pattern-designers a better knowledge of forms and of the proper combination of colors.

Much more in the same direction is wanted; but I have no hesitation in ascribing a considerable part of our past success in the production of fancy goods to the influence of these schools, and cannot but believe that equal, or even greater or more lasting, benefits would be derived from facilities being offered for the acquirement of the scientific knowledge of the principles which we have to carry into practice.

The fourth question involves the whole problem which now occupies so much of the public mind; and he would be a bold man who undertook to answer it categorically.

We are all anxiously waiting for the Report from the School Inquiry Commissioners, and for answers to a circular issued by Lord Stanley to her Majesty's Foreign Legations, with reference to technical education abroad.

After having obtained these documents, we shall be better prepared to study the whole question, and to form an opinion as to the system of technical education we may prefer.

But I believe, whatever may be the tenor of these reports, the people of Bradford will be confirmed in their opinion, that technical instruction not based upon a system of sound elementary and secondary education would not meet the wants of the country; and that government action in this matter ought to embrace the whole system of education, and not a part only.

In no other country has practical technical education been more perfect than in England; and the great number of most valuable inventions and improvements which have been made by uneducated workmen prove that this practical education has had excellent results.

I may also state that I am convinced that no school can ever give the same practical education as that which is given in the real workshop; but it is evident that in places like Bradford, where this branch of education is so thoroughly satisfactory, teaching of a more scientific character would be doubly beneficial.

To impart this necessary theoretical instruction, technical schools of different grades will be required; and as your lordship has asked the question, What kind of technical education we have to propose? I may be permitted to conclude with a few practical suggestions.

A polytechnic university like the Polytechnic School of Zurich, or the Central School at Paris, of which Mr. Samuelson gives so favorable an account, might be established in London, if a more central place in the kingdom be not preferred.

Three or four intermediate science and art colleges in different parts of the country, like the Écoles des Arts and Métiers in France, might prepare the young men from fourteen to eighteen years of age for the central university, or complete the education of those who do not intend to take degrees, or cannot aspire to the highest places in industrial professions.

Local institutions, such as weaving-schools, upon the Elberfeld model, with schools of art, lessons in chemistry, mechanics, and higher mathematics, might be spread over the whole country, each adapted to the industry of the district, and all connected with and aided by the superior schools and central university.

Evening classes might greatly assist the youths who have not yet obtained the benefit of those improvements in primary and secondary education, which, we trust, may not only give us more intelligent workmen and overlookers, but will afford to the rising generation in general that education which has so greatly assisted Germans and Swiss to become such dangerous competitors in the world's trade.

I have, &c.,

(Signed) JACOB BEHRENS.

To the Right Honorable the Lord Robert Montagu, M.P., Vice-President of the Committee of Council for Education, &c.

DECLINE OF SILK MANUFACTURE IN ENGLAND.

The following letter from Mr. Francis Beunoch to Mr. J. Hole shows that a lack of suitable technical education had much to do with the decline of silk manufacture in England.

80 WOOD STREET, E.C., Jan. 23, 1868.

DEAR SIR, — In reply to your letter and circular, received a few weeks ago, desiring me to note down any facts connected with the decline of the silk-trade in England, I feel obliged to embrace a wider range of view than the question at first sight might appear to render necessary.

Primarily, permit me to observe, that, although the French treaty may have *hastened* what has been almost a catastrophe in the silk manufacture, it had very little, if any thing, to do with the absolute decay. The skilled English operative is, in my opinion, quite as clever as the foreigner. The ignorance or incompetence exists where few suspect, — not in the worker or weaver, but in the master or employer. Protection fostered and pampered the trade, rendering a moderate profit possible and easy. But, when the competition became closer, ignorance succumbed to skill; for, unhappily, protection enabled many men to live by manufactures who knew little or nothing of manufacturing. I shall briefly notice the various stages; and, with the exception of the skilled weaver, I fear I shall have to condemn, or at all events criticise severely, and give little credit to, the trained ability manifested by those who profess to conduct the silk business.

Raw Material. — At the very outset, the English manufacturer is placed at a great disadvantage. No silk is produced at home: all must be imported. He relies, to a large extent, on China, Japan, and India, for his supply. The markets of France and Italy are opened to him; but there he is forestalled by the enterprising manufacturer of France, Switzerland, and Germany.

The English manufacturer chiefly depends for his supply upon the silk brought to London. The French, Swiss, and German manufacturers contract with the agents at Milan, or elsewhere, for a supply of the exact article required. Excellency of manufacture depends greatly on the evenness of the thread. In this respect the French and Italian silks are admirable. To secure this the greatest care is indispensable at the very first operation, — that of reeling from the cocoon. In all Asiatic silks, not only is this important process most negligently executed, but, when completed, the producer not only takes no heed as to keeping the several sizes apart, but brings to bear the utmost ingenuity to put together into the same hank several sizes, by reeling, first the coarsest, then a finer, and a finer still, until the coarse is completely enveloped in, or plated over, by a quality infinitely superior: so that the silk in this way may appear ten or twenty per cent better than it really is.

To separate and re-divide such hanks, and arrange them in exact sizes, is next to impossible. The remedy for this must be applied at the fountain-head. But who is to do it? The importer of silk is not, or very seldom is, interested in silk manufactures: so long as he can obtain silk in exchange for his calicoes, shipped to the East upon terms that leave him a profit, he cares little how it is produced, or what becomes of it. With careful reeling, there is no reason why the excellent fibre of the Chinese silk should not rank with the best Italian.

What has been done once may be repeated with advantage. I remember the time when Brutia silk ranked very low in this market, lower than our ordinary China: but some enterprising men, accurately estimating the value of the fibre, arranged to have it reeled on the Italian or French system; and the result was, that a silk once lightly esteemed now ranks with the best French or Italian silks, and for lace purposes is preferred to any other. Taking a money criterion, a silk which stood so low, if reeled as formerly, would not now, in this market, be worth more than twenty-one to twenty-four shillings, is at present worth forty-four to forty-eight shillings per pound.

This very year supplies a further argument in favor of the advantage of careful reeling. There have been great variations in the quantity imported; but it is found to be so irregular and badly reeled that it cannot be used with advantage in the fabrics most in demand. The consequence is, that, whereas French and Italian silks are even higher in price than they were a year ago, Asiatic silks are lower by twenty to twenty-five per cent. Here, one would think, is inducement enough for enterprising men to imitate a wiser system. But again I ask, Who is to do it? No substantial improvement in this respect can take place until the importer or merchant, and manufacturer or consumer, come closer together, and work with or for each other. At present they are kept apart, and are ignorant of each other, by a system that damages both. Did the manufacturer come in contact with the merchant, and fully discuss his requirements, the merchant would, for his own advantage, duly advise his agent in China or Japan, who would instruct the native producer; and so, in a short time, the evil pointed out might be partially amended, if not entirely overcome.

THROWING. — The throwster, again, is a middle-man; occasionally, but not always, a manufacturer. His business is to take the silk as imported, split up the skeins into their appropriate sizes, wind, twist, and prepare the silk for the manufacturer. This is the second and most important process; and carelessness on his part, or want of skill in separating and arranging the sizes, must be shown in the manufactured goods.

His work is delicate and difficult, and, I must admit, conducted with little notion as to his responsibility.

The general custom is, that, for a certain price per pound-weight, he undertakes to throw the silk into organzine, or tram, or warp and weft, and return the same weight. Thus if the throwster receives a hundred pounds silk, valued at thirty shillings per pound, he throws it, and whatever it produces (say ninety-five pounds of thrown silk) with five pounds waste, which he returns to the dealer at 33*s.* 6*d.*; the 3*s.* 6*d.* being the amount agreed to cover the charge for throwing, including waste. Here, you will observe, lies a great temptation, which few are able to resist.

In the best silks, the natural gum forms from eighteen to twenty-four per cent: this natural gum must be boiled out before the silk can be properly dyed. To secure himself a better profit, the throwster takes out as little of the foul or rough thread as possible, though every rough thread makes an imperfection in the web; in addition to which he will increase the quantity of soap used to soften the gum and make the silk more easy to wind, and, by leaving a portion of this adhering to the silk, he may lessen the difference in the raw silk received and the thrown silk returned, by two or three per cent. Indeed, so skilful have some throwsters become in this respect, that they can not only return the full weight received, but have some to spare, although five per cent to ten per cent must go in waste during the many processes through which the silk is put in the course of throwing.

I have frequently known instances when silk lost in boiling off from thirty per cent to thirty-five per cent in gum, soap, and other abominations; though the natural gum did not exceed twenty per cent to twenty-two per cent.

Mark the result: no really first-rate manufacturer on the Continent will look at English thrown silk for high-class goods. I freely admit, that, among the throwsters, there are many skilled and honorable men; but they have little influence to counteract the prevailing feeling, which is not a prejudice, but a principle. Men do not like to pay thirty shillings or forty shillings per pound for soap worth only sixpence per pound.

All this is destructive to our reputation as producers of prepared material, and most damaging to our home manufacturers, who, to a large extent, depend upon the English throwster for their supply of material. With material so prepared, what reasonable being could expect excellency of result?

Dyeing. — We have some very good practical dyers, but few who have been scientifically trained in chemistry. The consequence is, that, even in *black*, large quantities of silk are sent, at very heavy expense, every year to the Continent to be dyed, returned to Spitalfields, Coventry, Derby, Manchester, &c., to be woven, — a fact most discreditable to the dyers of England, and a great disadvantage to the manufacturer.

Manufacturing. — Here I take up the observations made at the outset, — very few of our manufacturers have any true technical training. To a great extent, they depend upon help supplied in the shape of a foreman, who has probably been a weaver, and knows something of putting silk together, but very little of the nature or inherent quality of silk, yet is made responsible for selecting a silk which *he thinks may* answer in producing a class of goods which his master has decided to make. A certain kind of silk has produced certain results before; and they think it probable that the silk offered them by the dealer may do the same again. And (in Coventry, for instance) it is frequently handed in bulk, so much organ, so much tram, with instructions to make the material into such and such goods; and they see no more of it until it is returned in the manufactured state. How can that be called manufacturing? The uncertainty as to the size of the material they use, and the ultimate result, renders it almost impossible for the professed manufacturer to estimate what the cost is of any given article until it is produced; whereas the foreign manufacturer, by the absolute knowledge of every department of his business, the reliance he can place on his material, and his skill in design, is enabled, after a careful examination of almost any pattern that can be laid before him, to give an estimate of cost within one or two per cent.

Instead of continuing the unpleasant task of showing what the English manufacturer cannot do, I shall endeavor to depict or describe the training necessary to make an accomplished manufacturer; and, in doing so, I shall not draw on my imagination, but keep steadily in view examples of men who have pursued a similar course of training. One of the great obstacles to success in silk manufactures in England is pride, as if being a manufacturer was an absolute degradation. It is not so on the Continent.

When the usual course of education is finished, and the young man has to determine, or his friends have to determine for him, what his future career is to be, his studies are regulated accordingly. If a manufacturer, he attends classes and lectures on natural science, with special reference to the branch of manufacture he intends to prosecute, — whether wool, linen, cotton, or silk, and does not waste his time on much discursive study. He studies the different kinds of silk, ascertains their nature, what classes of goods they are beneficially adapted for, and what they are not: so that, when he comes to practical working, he knows to a certainty what to reject, and what to select for his purpose. Along with this he prosecutes the study of chemistry, and, by experiments, learns what class of silk is best adapted for certain colors, and what is not. Equipped with this indispensable fundamental knowledge, he proceeds to Italy, or elsewhere, and practically engages in reeling from the cocoon: by and by he enters a throwing establishment, and becomes acquainted with every detail. In future life he can not only describe what he requires, but how it may be accomplished; for the ultimate result depends much more on the character and exactness of the several processes than many would suppose. Armed with this knowledge, he returns, and studies the art of design, and how best to produce a desired effect without the waste of a thread of material, and probably, for a year or so, practically studies weaving, and becomes a weaver at the loom. He is thus able personally not only to superintend, but practically carry out, every scheme his imagination can suggest.

With judgment so matured, and knowledge so complete, it requires no depth of reasoning to decide how easy would be the victory of such a man over the untrained manufacturers of England.

I will only describe one process to show the difference between the practice in Basle and Coventry. In Basle, when the warp is completed, it is arranged ready for the loom, stretched over and between two beams, and carefully examined. Every nib, knot, and rough part is removed from the threads, so that, when in the loom, the weaver drives along merrily. The shuttle seldom, if ever, ceases through imperfection in the warp. Whilst in Coventry, the silk is warped and put into the loom as it comes from the dyer; and, while the weaver is picking and cleaning his warp before it comes to the *bâton*, he not unfrequently has one or two pickers or cleaners behind the loom, removing the rough part from the threads, with many stoppages and delays in the process of weaving. Any one may see that the one is clumsy and primitive, whilst the other is characterized by common sense, skill, and considerable economy.

No man can pretend to show that the weavers of Lyons, St. Etienne, Zurich, Basle, or Crefeld, are superior to those of Spitalfields, Coventry, Norwich, Manchester, and Macclesfield; but any one who would venture to maintain an equality of skill, practical and mechanical knowledge, on the part of our manufacturers, would only expose his ignorance of the facts so easily acquired by all who wish to obtain them.

In many respects the Swiss have carried their technical knowledge a step beyond the French. What but the personal skill of the manufacturer could have enabled Zurich, in many classes of goods, to successfully compete with Lyons, or Basle to rival St. Etienne? These are facts which cannot be gainsaid; and we cannot but lament the supineness, or want of pluck, in our manufacturers, who lazily permit a most beautiful branch of industry to be taken from us.

Those who call for protection seek to protect, not trade, but ignorance and idleness.

Take one instance. Immense quantities of spun silk are produced in England, sent to the Continent, made into ribbon-velvets, and returned to England in quantities almost beyond belief. The mere expense of carriage and expenses of various kinds cannot be estimated at less than ten per cent. Here is protection enough to stimulate enterprise; and yet, of the hundreds of thousands of pounds' value of velvets imported annually, scarcely a piece is made in England. What is the reason? Nothing but the want of well-trained, practical scientific mechanical skill. If the French Treaty had been the cause of distress in Coventry, St. Etienne would necessarily be in a state of high prosperity; but it is not so. St. Etienne is as badly off as Coventry, so far as ribbons are concerned. Basle, by superior technical skill and great economy, has beaten St. Etienne, as well as Coventry; and, while these ancient cities are in a state of collapse, Basle seems to enjoy a high tide of successful industry.

As regards Coventry, fashion has much to do with its great depression. While women wear doyleys, or small mats, on their heads, the ribbon trade must languish. But that has little to do with the general question ; and you may gather from what I have stated, that we have, in my judgment, small hopes of recovering our prestige in any branch of silk manufacture, until importers, throwsters, dyers, and manufacturers will each and all earnestly resolve to acquire all technical knowledge connected with the trade, and, working together, determine to apply it.

It would be unjust to close these hurried notes without stating most emphatically, that combinations among the men, and the determination of a small set of workmen to establish trade-lists, or prices, was the beginning of the decay of our silk manufactures. I have personally had instances where many thousands of pounds' value of goods were ordered on the Continent because of some small, wretched, technical objection on the part of the weaver, or of his tyrant, the Trade Union, because it seemed to interfere with a trade-list in Coventry. My memory supplies me with one case where an order was declined, although the weaver could have made over forty shillings a week wages, had the price offered been accepted ; the result being, that, in one season, more than twenty thousand pounds' worth of goods was ordered on the Continent which might have been produced in England.

Perfect freedom to employ or dispose of labor is an indispensable element for the future success of the silk-trade in England.

I am, &c.,

FRANCIS BEUNOCH.

FRENCH TESTIMONY.

By imperial decree, June 22, 1863, a large and able commission was appointed to inquire into the character of technical instruction throughout France. Some thirty different persons, whose evidence it was thought would be most valuable,—professors, heads of colleges, and manufacturers,—were summoned before the commission. The abstract of evidence taken by the commission, and the report it made June 20, 1865 (Gen. A. Morin, reporter), were deemed so valuable by the British Government, that a translation of the same was made and presented to both houses of parliament by command of her Majesty. Extracts will be given in different parts of this volume.

In his evidence, M. Girardon, founder and director of the Central School at Lyons, professor at La Martinière School, a free technical school, says:—

> "The majority of the pupils of La Martinière succeed in the careers in life which they select. There are in the town of Lyons a large number of skilled artisans who have sat on the benches of the school. The principal dyers are old pupils of the school; and to them is due the increased prosperity of the trade of the town by the remarkable discovery of the new and fashionable colors. The Polytechnic School has also received many of the pupils; and it is to their first success in La Martinière that they owe the brilliant position they have obtained,—a just recompense of their assiduity."

The evidence of M. Houel, manager of the Derosne establishment of Cail and Company, contains some things not directly pertinent to this chapter; but, as the directly pertinent parts cannot be readily separated from the rest, the whole is given. M. Houel says: —

"I shall commence with the question of the instruction of apprentices. I believe that in the principal centres of industry, as Lille or Mulhouse, more favorable conditions could be created than at Paris. Thus at Fives, at the establishment of Parent, Schaken, Caillet, and Company, of which I am the fourth partner, we have begun to give special instruction to our apprentices; and, doing this in the interest of the children and in that of the parents, we believe that it is also in the interest of our establishment.

"In fact, the provincial workshops are under quite different conditions from those in the capital. At Paris, as many workmen as are wanted can be found: in the provinces, on the contrary, it is often difficult. We are compelled to create a staff of employés and operatives, who, we wish, may become attached to our establishment: we must attract both children and parents by making it easy for them to find dwelling-places and schools close to their work. This is what we wish to effect, and in which we have already succeeded in many centres.

"Our establishment, founded now about three years, employs fifteen hundred to eighteen hundred men: we have sixty apprentices; and we are thinking of raising the number to three hundred or four hundred. Our apprentices have one hour of intellectual labor; but we believe, that, to learn properly, they should have four or five hours daily. We would willingly allow it to them; and we should probably arrive at an instruction which would qualify some of them to become candidates for the schools of arts and trades, and that under conditions very favorable to their practical knowledge.

"It has sometimes been spoken of to make workmen study at night: I believe that to be almost impossible. A man that has been at work all day cannot study, unless, indeed, he has an exceptional constitution. A man who has the care of a family, who works at piece-work, and gives all his energy to it, has need of the evening for rest. According to my idea, the working-man cannot gain much by studying at night: he may go to his class one evening, but he will not go again. It is the apprentice with whom we should occupy ourselves, because he is of an age to divide his time between manual and intellectual labor.

"Now-a-days it is necessary to have educated workmen. France sends as many artisans abroad as Fngland. When we have a workman to send to Italy or Spain, we inquire what he knows, and we find, that, in general, he is a thoroughly practical man, who knows his work perfectly; but if we ask him to make a calculation, or to keep an account of petty cash, we directly discover his incapacity. On the other hand, if we take a pupil from the schools, we find him less practical than the working-man, less able, on the whole, to meet the requirements of the situation. In fact, we are compelled to send, in preference, a man who is not educated, but who knows how to work. What is wanting, then, is a man capable of working, yet instructed; and it is therefore of the greatest importance to trade to promote the instruction of apprentices by attaching a school to the workshop, as we have done at Fives.

"I confess I have here given utterance to an idea which deserves to be considered practically. It would be well to examine in detail what are the cases where a child, giving six hours of work a day to his master, can be replaced by another child while the first one goes to school. There are circumstances under which there would be some difficulty in making apprentices thus alternately go to work;

but I think, that, in most cases, it would be possible. Thus, in a workshop like ours, I do not see why we could not employ two hundred apprentices, as well as thirty or forty: in fact, the majority merely work as assistants to the workmen, and could easily be replaced in this work by others. It is only when a child has himself commenced a piece of work, that it cannot be finished by another. But I think that this difficulty can be overcome by having twice as many children as are wanted for their work, and by giving each of them only half of what he can do in twelve hours.

"I think, then, that it would be an excellent plan to organize in one large industrial establishment an intellectual training sufficiently advanced to allow of practical and scientific acquirements being placed on the same footing, and to enable parents who are sufficiently enlightened to send their children to the schools of arts and trades. For my own part, I know of no better instruction to make able workmen than that which is given at those schools, because there the studies run parallel to one another. We are indebted to them for the fact, that, in mechanical construction, we are the equals of any other nation in Europe. We ourselves employ a great number of the pupils of these schools. Of the three hundred who pass out of them every year, there are some who are more or less not so well prepared; there are some of whom we can make nothing but workmen, sometimes even only moderately good workmen: but there are others who are very intelligent, and have profited to the utmost by the intellectual and scientific training they have received. Such as have not been able to learn mathematics, but possess practical capabilities, become excellent foremen. We meet with men among them who have a great liking for practical acquirements, because in general they are good draughtsmen. A young man who can work well, and is skilful with his hands, is also a good draughtsman; and that is one of the first qualifications of a good foreman.

"We are all the more in a position to feel the want of workmen who have a knowledge of drawing, in that our method of manufacture (which we owe to the schools of arts and trades) is quite different from that adopted in England, and from that which, for a long time, was in use in France. I am the manager of two works, — those of Messrs. Cail and Company, and those of Messrs. Parent, Schaken, Caillet, and Company, which employ together about five thousand hands. That number might be easily increased to fifty thousand, if we had a sufficiency of draughtsmen. Our method consists in giving full details of every work, piece by piece: so that the workman has only to execute the piece according to the drawings which are confided to him. With a large staff of draughtsmen we produce works at these establishments to the amount of over thirty millions of francs, which would be an impossibility without our means and process of maufacture.

"It must be acknowledged, that, in large workshops, apprentices are not in such favorable circumstances for learning their trades as in smaller ones. Establishments with large capital undertake considerable contracts, and are therefore compelled to make many things of the same description. In a small workshop, on the contrary, where they execute a variety of works, the same objects are not turned out in so large a number. We manufacture in our three establishments a hundred and fifty locomotives; and we could make two hundred: there are therefore many parts which are repeated. If a young man executes well a piece of work which is intrusted to him, it may happen that he has given to him the same work for a year or more; and he will be able to make a profit by it. In a pecuniary point of view, it is at once the interest of his employers, of his parents, and of himself, that he should continue for some time manufacturing the same thing.

"In the schools of arts and trades, this method is not adopted. There the pupils are made to execute works which are gradually made more and more difficult, so that their acquirements may increase gradually. But this mode of instruction has also its inconveniences; for the result is, that the pupils cannot produce their work rapidly. They ought to execute in these schools a greater quantity of work, and to have among the pupils a number of skilled mechanics to show them how to turn out their work quickly. We take every year fifteen pupils from the school at Châlons; and, as they are much sought after, we do our best to obtain the best. For two years they are employed in our workshops, and are then sent into the drawing-office: at the end of four or five years, they are of great service to us. But it is evident, that, if they were more conversant with manual labor when they leave school, they would not have to pass two years in the workshop: they could be spared that probation, and would be sooner in a position to occupy higher posts. Works of greater importance ought to be executed in the schools; and if, by the side of the pupils, there were a few picked workmen who knew how to turn out work well, they would serve as an example to the young men of the school; and those who possessed industry and ability would endeavor to emulate them in rapidity of execution and skill."

A sub-commission investigated and reported on technical education in Germany and Switzerland. Of the prosperity of Nuremberg this sub-commission says:—

"There exist in Germany certain institutions, all having for their object, though differing in form, the professional training (properly so called) of workmen. Foremost among the things taught in these schools, or classes, which are held on Sundays or evenings, always stands freehand and linear drawing. In some countries, as in Wurtemberg and Bavaria (Nuremberg), drawing is the especial object of these schools; and the impulse it has given to all the industries requiring that art are sufficiently striking, and so generally recognized as to render evident the usefulness and necessity of this branch of instruction.

"A glance at the immense variety of children's toys with which Nuremberg supplies the whole world will suffice to show the progress due to this diffusion of the art of drawing. The very smallest figures, whether men or animals, are all produced with almost artistic forms; and yet all these articles are made in the cottages of the mountainous districts of the country. They find employment for the whole population, from children of tender age, as soon as they can handle a knife, to their parents; and this home manufacture, which does not interfere with field-work, contributes greatly to the prosperity of a country naturally poor and sterile."

The same sub-commission, in giving an historical account of the schools of arts and trades in France, tells the following anecdote of the first Napoleon, which indicates the value he placed upon technical education: —

"One day the emperor, while still first consul, paid a visit to the college at Compiégne, and questioned some of the elder pupils as to what they intended to do on leaving the college. He was much dissatisfied with their answers. 'The government,' said he, 'pays considerable sums to educate these young men; and, when their studies are ended, none of them, except those who enter the army, are of any use to the country. Nearly all of them remain at home, a burden to their families, which they ought to aid. This shall continue no longer. I have just visited the great manufacturing establishments in the north, and the larger workshops of Paris. I everywhere found foremen clever in the manual labor of their trades, but scarcely one among them able to draw the outlines, or make the most simple calculations, of a machine to convey his ideas by a sketch or a written description. This is a great defect; and I will here provide the means for remedying it. There must be no more Latin here (that will be learned in the lyceums about to be organized), but the study of trades, with so much theory as is necessary for their progress: by this course we shall obtain well-taught foremen for our manufactories."

VIEWS OF PROF. LEONI LEVI.

Prof. Leoni Levi, Doctor of Economic Science of the University of Tübingen, having investigated technical, industrial, and professional instruction in Italy and other countries, made a report to Lord Montagu, the vice-president of the Committee of Council on Education in Great Britain. This Report was ordered by the House of Commons to be printed, Dec. 6, 1867. After describing the instruction in different countries, Prof. Levi says: —

"This is but a general review of what is being done with a view to promote scientific and technical instruction in different countries, yet it is sufficient to show that the greatest attention is devoted to the subject; that a general desire is evinced to advance in industry, not by the empirical method of chance acquisitions, but by a profound study of the great principles of art and science; that experimental science is attracting an extensive number of laborers, intent upon making fresh discoveries and greater conquests over the grand and mysterious powers of matter; and that the exercise of the different professions of life is no longer left in the hands of persons untaught and undisciplined, but is everywhere made to depend on an extended knowledge of the sciences which they demand, and of the duties which they impose.

"What is done in this country towards promoting objects of such paramount importance? The principal defect in popular education in this country, I apprehend, is a want of elevation of mind and of capacity of exercising force or power of thought. There appears to be a want of agility and adaptability in the mental powers of our working-classes, produced, probably, by the early ages at which they are sent to work, the hardness, constancy, and sameness of labor, and by the dull and unenlivening climate. In the constant use of machinery, the laborers in the manufacturing districts become, to a great extent, the slaves of mechanical force, and, bound to follow the automaton by a constantly watchful eye, they lose that vivacity of mind which is necessary to the efficient pursuit of every branch of industry. Nor have the majority of laborers much opportunity to acquire an intelligent knowledge of the work they have to do.

"The only means generally provided for learning the work is by the system of apprenticeship; but, in the hurry and turmoil of the workshop, no attention is paid to the principles of the work. By constant practice, by great care, by natural aptitude, the laborer may acquire an unrivalled excellence of workmanship; his eye may be so sharpened, and his touch so refined, as to be able to detect the most infinitesimal flaw in the work at hand: but ask him to alter his course, or to introduce any novelty, and he is utterly incompetent for it. This is the effect of apprenticeship unaided by any study of the principles involved in the art. The laborer is, in fact, reduced to the character of a copying-machine: he may be able to transcribe what is set before him with the utmost perfection, but cannot at any time alter, invent, or even skilfully control, what is to be done. He is rather the slave than the master of the work he has on hand. What the laborer really wants is a knowledge of the principles on which the work is done. It is not desirable to substitute science for practice; but it would be most useful to superadd the one to the other. It is not a question of abolishing the system of apprenticeship for the school, but to let the school be preparatory to or the immediate attendant of apprenticeship."

REPLIES TO LORD STANLEY.

In 1867 Lord Stanley addressed a circular to her Majesty's ministers abroad, requesting them to obtain and forward information relating to technical or industrial education in foreign countries.

1. What is the nature of any technical or industrial education which is carried on in ——? What are the particular industries which it is intended to promote? Are there any distinct schools or colleges, &c., for the purpose?

2. If there be such schools or colleges, with what industries are they connected?

3. For what class of persons is this technical instruction adapted? — for masters, overlookers, or workmen?

4. In what way are these institutions supported? and particularly do they receive any contribution from public funds, as endowments, subsidies from local or central authorities?

5. What is the average number of the students?

6. What is the cost to a student? Are there any exhibitions or free places tenable at industrial schools, &c.? Do private manufacturers often defray the expenses of students?

7. Is there any special qualification required for admission to the industrial school, &c.? What is the time usually spent by students at the schools, &c., and the ages and sex of the students?

8. What is the amount of the education presumed, or generally acquired, before admission to the school, &c.? What are the subjects of instruction at the school, &c.? What is the mode in which instruction is given? Is the instruction accompanied by participation in actual manufacturing works or processes?

9. Are there any special privileges attached to studentship at the school, &c.? Is any special education

of this kind made necessary for admission to the exercise of any particular trade or profession?

10. How are the teachers appointed? What qualifications are they required to have? How are these qualifications ascertained? and how obtained by those who possess them?

11. What advantage, if any, has resulted from these schools, &c., in promoting or extending the manufactures with which they are connected?

12. What is the opinion prevalent among the industrial classes, whether employers or employed, with regard to the working and effect of these schools?

In 1868 the replies were presented to both houses of parliament by her Majesty's command. With his reply relative to France, Lord Lyons sent numerous documents, — one a circular letter dated April 6, 1868, which was sent out by the minister of public instruction in France. It accompanied a plan of studies for the special schools. In this letter the French minister says of Switzerland, —

"Science continues its discoveries, and every day places at the disposal of industry new and serviceable agents; but, in order to be well applied, these agents, which are sometimes very delicate and sometimes very powerful, require to be skilfully handled. This is the reason why, in the present day, industrial progress is so intimately connected with educational progress, and why questions which it is the duty of the university to examine and to solve have acquired so great an importance even as regards the material prosperity of France.

"Should any one doubt the importance of the revolution which is taking place, let him look at Switzerland, that country of lakes and mountains, which Nature has made so beautiful, while at the same time denying it every condition required to make it the abode of industry, — a country loved by artists and by poets, but without ports, without navigable rivers, without canals, and without mines. Yet, from among these sterile rocks, there is exported every year an amount of products sufficient to pay for all the importations made, and more especially for the two hundred million francs' worth of goods which France alone sells to that people, which in former times cultivated mercenary warfare as its sole branch of industry; and the country produces, besides, so many skilful men, that, in every commercial city of the world, a Swiss colony is found holding the first rank; and in almost every great commercial house may be found intelligent clerks who have come from Basle, Zurich, or Neufchâtel."

Mr. Lowther, in his reply from Berlin, speaks thus of the general effect of technical instruction in Prussia: —

"The advantage obtained is, that there has been a very good class of workmen established, which *thinks*, and has a knowledge of the things they are required to make, and consequently comprehends more easily. The class of workmen has become also better mannered, more civilized and refined. The middle class of tradespeople has been able to raise the profession: it has been able to carry into effect all repairs in factories, and to arrange and direct them in such a way that they are cared for in the most convenient manner. It has been able to introduce new methods in manufactories, &c. The highest education of German engineers has caused the profession to be very much sought after on account of its extensive and fundamental knowledge. By means of all these circumstances, Prussian establishments, like Prussian industry, have been able to raise themselves.

"The industrial classes have the most favorable opinion of this education, as proved by the very great use made of all the technical places or establishments of education of all grades, &c., as proved by the necessary enlargement of existing, and formation of new, establishments. The workmen feel the influence of the knowledge they have acquired, and are anxious to attend the lectures at the *vereins* (unions), which conduce to show the workman the importance of theory. From ten thousand to twelve thousand men attend the lectures of the *Handwerker Verein* at Berlin alone.

"Looking at the result given in answer to Question 5, that about eleven thousand men receive a technical education annually in various grades of knowledge, it will easily be understood that the effects of these technical establishments of education are generally recognized."

Mr. Doria sends with his report from Stockholm a communication from the Swedish Government, which says of the technical schools in Sweden:—

"The facts that the number of persons who seek admission into the schools is constantly increasing, and that manufacturers and others engaged in industrial pursuits exert their influence in every diet to promote the increase or extension of technical educational establishments, are sufficient proof that the use of such schools is evident to the public, and duly appreciated."

Of the good effect of the many industrial and technical schools in Belgium, Lord Howard de Walden says:—

"The benefits which these institutions have conferred, and are conferring, upon the working population of Flanders, as regards their material prosperity, in resuscitating a decayed industry, and in opening a career of renumerative labor to all who are willing to avail themselves of the opportunity placed within their reach, whilst teaching them, at the same time, early habits of discipline and order, are incontestable."

With his reply, Lord Howard de Walden sent an elaborate report on industrial education in Belgium made by the minister of the interior in 1867. This report gives an account of a large number of local technical schools. Of the good influence of the one at Soigneis, specially designed for workers in stone quarries, and in which great attention is paid to drawing, the minister says:—

"The school has a good influence upon the working-class, and upon the industry of the town of Soigneis and the neighborhood. It provides this industry with efficient powers and skilled workmen, who work the stone with taste, and execute the most complicated work, and, above all, remarkable carvings, which the owners of the quarries could hardly undertake before, or which they were obliged to have executed elsewhere. On the other hand, it provides the pupils with knowledge which enables them to improve their condition considerably. It also acts favorably on their morality, giving them a taste for study, and ideas of order and providence which contribute to the spread of well-being and competency in families."

TESTIMONY OF MR. SAMUELSON.

Mr. Bernhard Samuelson, member of parliament, having made a tour of observation, wrote a letter, Nov. 16, 1867, on the industrial progress, and the education of the industrial classes, in France, Switzerland, Germany, &c. This letter, addressed to the vice-president of the Committee of Council for Education in Great Britain, was ordered by the House of Commons to be printed. Of woollen manufactures Mr. Samuelson says: —

" In contrasting what I saw at Leeds and the older seats of the woollen manufacture with the worsted spinning and weaving factories at Bradford, I had no difficulty in comprehending how it happens that Continental competition is being far more seriously felt in the former than in the latter department of the woollen trade. In the woollen manufacture proper, every thing has stiffened into tradition and routine. The most enlightened and enterprising manufacturers are discouraged by the passive resistance of their old-fashioned overlookers and other 'leading hands.' Even in those cases where improved machinery is introduced, it is not used to the utmost advantage. One result is, that the spinners and manufacturers of Belgium are exporting woollen yarns and cloths, valued at nearly two million pounds, annually to this country, produced from wools, a great portion of which are first imported from our colonies and transatlantic countries, into London, and shipped thence to Antwerp. I was told by the president of the Leeds Chamber of Commerce that the discouragement arising from these conditions is so great, that the more enterprising young men refuse to engage in the woollen manufacture, and enter one or other of the numerous branches of industry which have recently sprung up in Leeds, and to which the maintenance of its prosperity is principally due.

"It is not surprising, under these circumstances, that the manufacturers of Leeds, through their Chamber of Commerce, should urge the necessity of giving a more free and scientific training to its rising generation.

"At Bradford all is different. The worsted manufacture, a comparatively young trade, is carried on with the newest appliances, in factories admirably designed, by master manufacturers of unsurpassed energy, and a working population free from the prejudices which, amongst ignorant people, are the unavoidable accompaniment of routine."

Of the good influence of art instruction on lace manufactures Mr. Samuelson observes : —

"To the general depression of the Nottingham lace-trade the manufacture of lace curtains forms an exception. To this branch, the admirable local school of art, the erection and fittings of which cost nearly eight thousand pounds, has rendered the greatest service. I saw some beautiful designs by pupils of the school, which were being executed in one of the factories; and I have been informed that the English patterns in this branch are preferred to those of France, not only in England, but in the markets of the world."

The following, from Mr. Samuelson, illustrates how rude labor may be supplanted by machinery, the product of skilled labor: —

"Apart from their general interest, the works of the Isthmus of Suez Canal (the beautiful drawings and models of which attracted so much attention in the Champ-de-Mars) afford an instance, which I cannot omit to notice, of the resources of French mechanical engineering. It will be remembered that the progress of this great undertaking was arrested about five years ago by the prohibition, on the part of the Porte, of forced labor. The contractors, finding themselves deprived of some eighteen thousand workpeople, at once reconsidered their plans, and proposed to substitute special steam-machinery of an entirely original character for the manual labor previously employed in excavating and embanking the main and fresh water canals and the entrance from the Mediterranean. Nearly the whole of that machinery, costing several millions sterling, was executed in France, — about six hundred thousand pounds' worth by Messieurs Gouin and Company of Paris. Within twelve months from the receipt of the order, these gentlemen prepared the plans of the dredges, barges, cranes, &c., and delivered and erected at Port Said a sufficient quantity of the material to commence the works; and within three years the whole of this enormous plant was completed, and in satisfactory operation. Monsieur Gouin is a pupil of the Polytechnic School; and Monsieur Lavallée, the contractor, to whose talent and energy the conception of these tools, and the resumption of the works, is due, a pupil of his late father at the École Centrale."

Mr. Samuelson thus describes the wonderful results

which have been achieved at Creuzot, France, by the technical education of the workmen and by perfect organization:—

"The works were founded in 1781, and dragged on a precarious existence until they were purchased by Messieurs Schneider, in 1836, after having been abandoned for several years. They are still the property of Monsieur Henry Schneider (president of the Corps Législatif), of his son, and a small number of other partners, with limited liability. When they passed into the hands of Messieurs Schneider, sixty thousand tons of coal were raised, and four thousand tons of iron produced annually; and there were no traces of the vast mechanical workshops whose magnificent products formed so remarkable a feature of the late Paris Exhibition.

"The works now cover three hundred acres; the workshops and forges, fifty acres; and the mines yield annually two hundred and fifty thousand tons of coal, and three hundred thousand tons of iron ore: three hundred thousand tons of coal, and about a hundred and twenty thousand tons of ores, are purchased. The iron-works produce more than a hundred thousand tons of iron, besides machinery, locomotive and marine, iron bridges and viaducts, and even iron gun-boats and river-steamers, of an average yearly value of six hundred thousand pounds. The pay-sheets return nine thousand nine hundred and fifty work-people, and wages amounting to three hundred and seventy thousand pounds per annum; and the steam-engines are equal to a duty of nearly ten thousand horse-power. These marvellous works have therefore been virtually created in thirty years; and, in fact, the well-built, well-paved town of Creuzot, with its churches, its schools, its markets, its gas and water works, and its handsome public walks, inhabited by nearly twenty-four thousand well-fed and decently-clad people, has taken the place of the wretched pit village of two thousand seven hundred inhabitants of 1836. There is no overcrowding; the space in the dwelling-houses averaging one thousand one hundred cubic feet per head of the population. Notwithstanding his public duties, Monsieur Schneider retains the chief direction of the works. During the session of the chamber, the immediate management on the spot is in the hands of his son; but, in the recess, he resides at Creuzot. After having conducted me for several hours through these vast works, Monsieur Schneider returned to his office to complete and despatch his correspondence, and debate the most minute economical points, items of cost, and rates of carriage, with the heads of departments; showing himself, as he expressed it, '*industriel jusqu'au bout des ongles.*' He will forgive me for entering into these personal details. They are interesting to France and to England, more especially to England, where high political duties are still deemed almost incompatible with an active industrial career.

"To describe the works in detail would carry me beyond the limits of this Report. I saw no new mechanical contrivances. The best English designs were followed; but no appliances for producing perfect work, or for economizing the cost of production, have been omitted; and the new forge contained under a single roof (a thousand three hundred feet in length and three hundred and ten feet in breadth) is probably unequalled in the world. A very large proportion of the *personnel* of every rank in this great establishment was born and has been trained on the spot; and the possibility of thus forming highly-skilled workmen, competent engineers and accountants, is due, in a great measure, to a system of education, dating back as far as 1841, which, though it is modestly styled elementary, is far more advanced and 'special' than the term implies. The course — not necessarily followed throughout by all, but open to all of sufficient capacity — extends over nine years, and includes advanced instruction in French literature, history, geography, natural philosophy, the chemistry of metals, algebra, geometry, mechanical and freehand drawing, and modelling. The more promising boys are sent to the secondary and higher technical schools; and many a Creuzot laborer's son may be found, who, having passed through the École des Arts et Métiers, at Aix, has returned to fill a responsible position in the technical management. The other boys are drafted from the school into the works, and placed there strictly according to the capacity which they have shown at school; some as simple workmen, others as accountants or as draughtsmen. Education is not compulsory; but no Creuzot boy is admitted into the works who cannot read and write, and none who has been turned out of school for misbehavior.

"No doubt many of the boys, as they grow up, unlearn much of what they have accquired. It is not in one generation that the most strenuous efforts in favor of education can be expected to bear ripe fruit; but a proof that they are not illusory as to the mass may be found in the fact, that whereas, amongst those employed at Creuzot, but coming from the villages or from a distance, thirty-one per cent of the conscripts, on the average of the last six years, were illiterate, only nine per cent of those born or brought up in the town were unable to read and write. There are adult classes, less as a corrective of deficient elementary instruction than as a help to those who wish to carry their studies beyond that of the school. They are held on Tuesday, Friday, and Sunday, and included, at the outset, reading, writing, arithmetic, geometry, natural philosophy, chemistry, geography, history, linear and freehand drawing, and music; but, of late years, six of the heads of departments, pupils of the École des Arts and Métiers, have been appointed to teach special classes, bearing directly on the occupations of the workmen, and including, as one of the most important, a complete course of machine drawing. Though the proportion of adult pupils here, as elsewhere, is small, — five per cent of the whole number of workmen, — the result is, that Monsieur Schneider, in walking through the sheds where several pairs of marine engines were being erected, was able to inform me that there was not a man amongst the mechanics employed in that department who could not make an accurate drawing of the work on which he was engaged.

"What this signifies and is worth, a mechanic alone can fully appreciate. Of the two hundred and sixty-eight superior engineers, managers, book-keepers, &c., a hundred and twenty-seven, or nearly one-half, were educated at Creuzot; five were pupils of the École Centrale; five, of the Imperial Mining School; twenty, of the three Écoles des Arts and Métiers; two, of the École la Martinière at Lyons; a hundred and four from various schools. Most of the latter, however, were of middle age, and entered Creuzot when its present system was still in process of creation. The schools which were opened in 1841 with ninety-one children contained 4,065 in 1866, of whom 2,219 were boys; the entire number of children in Creuzot between the ages of five and fifteen being 4,638 at the same period. There are eleven schoolmasters, under a chief director, in the boys' schools; and the girls are taught by eleven *sœurs*. The school-fees are seven pence per month for the children of persons employed in the works, and fourteen pence for those of strangers. Wages, though they have increased about one-half during the last twenty years, are still low compared with those to which we are accustomed. They amount, on the average of the entire establishment, to 2*s*. 10*d*. per day, including the unskilled laborers and boys. The average wages of those employed at the mines and coal-pits are 2*s.* 8*d.*; at the forges, 3*s.*; at the blast-furnaces, 2*s.* 3*d.*; and in the workshops, 2*s.* 9*d.*: but the more highly skilled mechanics will earn as much as 6*s.* 6*d.*, and the puddlers from 6*s.* to 9*s.* 6*d.* per day. The lowest wages of the latter, according to a pay-sheet exhibited in the forge at the time of my visit, were 5*s.* 6*d.*; and it is worthy of observation, that whilst, in nearly every other department, the working-staff is recruited amongst the children of the work-people, they are averse to the rude task of the puddling furnaces, in spite of the attraction of high pay: so that in this branch the labor is imported generally from the surrounding villages; boys being taken into the forge at the ages of sixteen and seventeen, when their frames are approaching maturity. But the tendency of modern improvements is to substitute mechanical and chemical processes for such work as that of puddling; and it will probably not be long before it is superseded. Meanwhile, the employment of children of tender years during the night is almost entirely dispensed with. Girls under seventeen are never admitted. Women do not work below the surface, as they do in Belgium; and the few females in the works, only four per cent of the whole, are employed in the light day-work of dressing ores, and similar occupations. Boys scarcely ever enter the works before fourteen. Every person is paid immediately by the proprietors, and nearly all by the piece or the ton. The ruinous system of contracts with middlemen, pursued in our iron works, is unknown. There are no "butties," no forge contractors earning their two pounds per day, no "underhands" paid by puddlers: the humblest laborer comes into personal contact with the managers; and his work is appraised by men of education, and paid for according to its relative value. Tables showing the actual daily earnings of every man are suspended in the workshops of the several departments, so as to be open to the inspection, and to stimulate the emulation, of all.

"In reference to the moral condition of the population, I will simply state, that, during fifteen years, the entire number of serious felonies in the town of Creuzot was twenty-three; but of these only nine would have been felonies according to our law. The number of misdemeanors was about forty annually; but many of these would not have constituted breaches of the law with us: amongst others, I may mention simple bankruptcy, maiming to escape military service, and abusive language. I was told that three policemen form the entire preventive force. Drunkenness is rare. I certainly did not observe a single case during my visit."

TESTIMONY OF ENGLISH ARTISANS.

Through the efforts of the English Council of the Society of Arts, sufficient money was secured, mainly by private subscription, to send more than eighty skilled workmen, representing almost as many industries, to study the Paris Exhibition, 1867, and to visit different parts of France for the examination of various workshops and manufacturing establishments. Each workman, upon his return, was required to furnish, and did furnish, a written report giving the result of his observations. To most of them report-writing was a novel labor; but their reports, compactly filling a volume of some seven hundred pages, form one of the most valuable contributions to the industrial literature of the day.

Mr. Thomas Connolly, stone-mason, says: —

"It is impossible to estimate the loss which is entailed upon England through the neglect of art culture in every department of our industry. Through it we are reduced to mere hewers of wood and drawers of water for other nations. The bulk of our able-bodied population is engaged in manufacturing goods to be sold cheap, or in producing raw materials for other people to work; while the more delicate portion have to subsist on their earnings for want of employments suitable to their strength. The streets of London and our large towns are torn up with heavy traffic, which is scarcely perceptible in Paris; for, if a ton of iron enters there (for which we may get less than a pound), they are sure to put a hundred pounds' worth of labor on it before it leaves their hands. . . .

"When a stone has to be worked to a mould, or fitted to a square or a straight-edge, no man can do it more workmanlike, or to a greater perfection, than an English mason; but, when the hands have to realize the imagination, the Frenchman's familiarity with art, and his early training in its principles, enable him to outstrip us; and, as every building in Paris is more or less decorated with carving, you are at a loss to know how they get all their art workmen. But the difficulty would not appear so much, if you could read the large placards, in French, which are posted up at the ends of the bridges and other public places, informing workmen where they can be taught drawing and modelling every evening free of expense. That he outstrips the Englishman in this respect does not, I feel certain, arise from the possession of an especial art genius, but because whatever of it is in him is fully developed, and encouragement is given to its practice; and, if English workmen are behind in this respect, it is not because art genius is deficient in our nature, but because it is not developed and encouraged sufficiently. . . .

"The French Exhibition has shown us that England is far behind in art manufacture; so that any suggestion for our improvement is worth considering. I believe the superiority of the French is owing to their education, and study of their business, both in and out of the workshop, to a greater extent than Englishmen."

Mr. W. T. Swene, practical superintendent of glass-works, Birmingham, says:—

"But I cannot refrain from once more pointing out the necessity that exists for art teaching; for we not only want skilled designers, but we want, in a greater degree, a knowledge of art on the part of our workmen. For how can a glass-blower who cannot draw the most simple curve be expected to have a correct eye for form, and true judgment in the proportions of the articles he is called upon to make? Or the glass-cutter similarly situated, how can he be expected to combine his decorations so as to improve, and not to spoil, the forms put into his hands? In the most important point, we may readily receive a great lesson from the Continental workers, who, while improving in a great degree in the quality and execution of their work, never lose sight of the importance of combining industrial skill with the application of art knowledge."

Mr. Benjamin Lucraft, chair-maker, says:—

"Not so with chairs of an artistic character: the lines are only a guide up to a certain point; and, from that point, the mere workman stands not the slightest chance with the workman of a cultivated

taste. The art workman of France has a great advantage over us in England. In Paris they are surrounded by works of that kind, which none but the most obtuse can long remain uninfluenced by. Their museums and palaces are central, and most numerous: their decorations and furniture are of the highest order, and nearly always open to the people. Even the Palace of Versailles, with its beautiful Louis Quatorze decorations, can be reached by rail as readily as I can reach South Kensington from my house at Islington. I mention these advantages the French enjoy, to show, to those who think climate and our plodding race have something to do with our want of taste, that there are other causes."

Mr. James Mackie, wood-carver, says: —

"Our great want is good designs, something that shall not be an unmeaning jumble, a more intelligent direction in carrying them out, a liberal use of thoroughly modelled works to be reproduced in the wood; and not till then shall we have a chance of reaching the goal side by side with other nations."

Mr. R. Baker, wood-carver, says: —

"In comparison with the French, the English carving is tame and spiritless. The French workman seems imbued with a true love of his art, and executes it with a warmth of feeling which gives it life and sentiment; and this gives his work its superiority. If we examine attentively a portion of French work, we find the main object of the carver is to give his work spirit and expression. Take a rose, for instance: it expresses all the characteristics of a rose: the form, the life, and even the color, is there substituted; and yet it is not the exact copy of the form of a rose, for, if it was, it would look poor and lifeless; but it looks rich, and full of life: and this is done with comparatively little labor. The carver must understand and feel the true spirit of the object he is carving, otherwise he may bestow much labor, and display much skill and cleverness in tooling; but his work will still be deficient in that which is essential to its artistic merit: not that there is a total absence of this artistic feeling in the English work; but they seem to have studied cutting their work sharp and clean, in preference to any thing else. As a whole, the English carving is equal, and perhaps superior, to any of their previous exhibitions. Their progress is seen not so much in what is actually exhibited, as in the almost entire absence of decidedly bad work. There are scarcely any of those tame and laborious imitations of nature which usually abound in our exhibitions. This indicates improvement in taste. . . .

"The French workman is generally supplied with good designs and models, which he slightly alters to suit the grain of his wood, without injuring the original design: this facilitates his progress. In fact, the employers seem to give their workmen every scope and encouragement for the display of their abilities."

Mr. Thomas Jacob, cabinet-draughtsman, says: —

"France is certainly before us in design, but not in workmanship. If steady hard labor or good sound workmanship is required, the English mechanic is second to none in the world, provided he has the tools and materials to work with; but, if art workmanship is required, it must come from a man, who, besides being a good mechanic, must, to some extent at least, be able to use the pencil also. This being the case, just as education proceeds, and a taste for the beautiful is diffused among workingmen generally, by means of schools of art and free access to our museums, particularly on Sundays, so will art workmanship in this country rise to at least a level with that which is so much admired abroad. . . .

"The French carvers do not work mechanically: invariably they make their own models to begin with, receiving only a rough sketch from the draughtsman; it being generally left to their taste to arrange it, so that they work in perfect freedom, with greater pleasure, and thus perfection."

Mr. L. S. Booth of Coventry, reporting on ribbons, says:—

"The ribbons, as a whole, are artistic in design, harmonious in color, and perfect in workmanship. No painter ever put color on canvas, and made those colors appear like real fruit or flowers, with bloom and every variety of tint, with more success than have the varied artisans engaged in this trade done. The productions are perfect specimens of their kind; in which the artist has brought all his varied power to imitate nature in form, the chemist in hue and color, and the artisan judgment and skill to work the whole, and make a success. Nor should it be forgotten, that, in producing these patterns, there has been an enormous outlay by the manufacturer for design, draught, and cards.

"To look at these articles in detail, we must begin with those produced in France, the first by way of order and also excellence."

Mr. John Randall, china-painter, says:—

"When we come to high-class ornamentation in iron, earthenware, china, or glass, the superiority of French art is obvious. As long as we confine ourselves to geometrical forms in hammering, pressing, turning on the lathes, or printing on the surface, we have no difficulty in holding our own; but where an intellectualism is concerned, or a free educated hand is required in decoration, our deficiencies become apparent. The fault is less our own than our rulers', who have denied us education, or who have, at least, given us nothing to fit us for our destinations in life, but have left us groping in the dark, forever feebly attempting to overtake lost opportunities."

TESTIMONY OF J. SCOTT RUSSELL.

Mr. J. Scott Russell, the builder of "The Great Eastern," is one of the most justly eminent authorities on the education of the working-classes. From his book, "Systematic Technical Education of the English People," the following extracts are made: —

"It is shown how easily education might double the value of the work done, of the profit reaped, and of the wages received. Twenty-five pounds represents the actual cost in education of a highly skilled over a skilless workman: in other words, the cost of producing a skilled workman is less than one year's purchase of his increased value to the nation. . . .

"It is notorious that those foreign railways which have been made by themselves in the educated countries of Germany and Switzerland have been made far cheaper than those constructed by us in England: it is known that they have been made by pupils of the industrial schools and technical colleges of these countries; and I know many of their distinguished men who take pride in saying that they owe their positions entirely to their technical schools. I find everywhere throughout their work marks of that method, order, symmetry, and absence of waste, which arise from plans well thought out, the judicious application of principles, conscientious parsimony, and a high feeling of professional responsibility. In the accurate cutting of their slopes and embankments, in the careful design and thoughtful execution of their beautiful but economical stone-masonry, in the self-denying economy of their large span bridges, the experienced traveller can read as he travels the work of a superiorly educated class of men; and when we come down to details, to the construction of permanent way, arrangements of signals, points, and sidings, and the endless details of stations, we everywhere feel that we are in the hands of men who have spared no pains, and who have applied high professional skill to minute details. . . .

"It seems to me almost an axiom, that intelligent men must do better work than boors; that trained, skilled men must do better work than clumsy and awkward ones; and that the more any man knows of the objects and methods of his own work, and of the work of all those who around him are engaged in co-operation, the more likely he is to do his own part well, and so as to make it exactly fit into and form one with his neighbor's work. Thus I think that an intelligent community of workmen will get through their work quicker, will fit the parts more nicely, will finish off every thing more sharply, will waste less material by trial and error, and so give higher value, as well as quality and durability, to all their work, than ignorant, unrefined, ill-educated men. . . .

"An important but perhaps not an obvious result of the systematic technical education of men of every class trained together in the same schools, colleges, and university, would be a transference of the same organization from the school to the workshop, and an amount of good understanding between all fellow-workers, which cannot fail to lighten individual labor, to save much waste of pains, materials, and thought, and to give great unity and perfection to the work done. The master being only a degree better educated and instructed than his foreman, it is plain that less pains will be required to make him understand what he is to undertake and do, and how he is to set about and do it; and thus the master's work will be all the easier, and his anxiety about its satisfactory execution all the less. Next, the foreman or leading workman will be only a little more able and better informed than the men under him, and only a little less skilled than his master, so that he can easily make his wishes known to those who have so much knowledge in common. The men, on the other hand, are perfectly prepared by their education and skill to comprehend the aim of their work, and its relation to the materials and the processes of which they are masters.

"Here, then, is produced by community of education that variety of co-operation by which the greatest and noblest works can be executed in the best and highest way.

"Where, on the contrary, workmen, superintendents, masters, have all received independent training, and come from classes of society kept apart from each other, even in their elementary education, the workman more or less illiterate, the master perhaps a scholar, but unskilled in work, it is plain, that, for some time at least, they will be kept far asunder by want of common ground for sympathy. To remedy this evil, the workman should have had a higher education, the master a more technical training; but, in the absence of these, what generally happens is a cure which perpetuates and exaggerates the distance between them. A middle-man steps in between the two, — sometimes he is a contractor for the labor of the men, — who says to the master, 'I know the nature of the men and their work; give me the money you have set aside, and I will see that they do the work, and undertake that it is done for the money.' He takes care, of course, that he himself is well paid. The wider the distance between master and men, the larger the margin for his profit; it becomes his interest that this margin shall grow: hence his skill is devoted to diminishing the wages of the workman and the profits of the masters. To the men he complains that the master is a screw; to the master he complains that the men won't work. Thus between uneducated men and unskilled masters a breach is made, ever growing wider and deeper. At the root of much of the system of combination of men against masters will be found to lie this primary incongruity of knowledge and ignorance, skill and unskill; and from it an alienation of interests ever growing, and always fostered by meddling middle-men, who at last become an indispensable but baleful element, beginning with conciliation, and ending with alienation. It matures into class distinction of the worst sort, continually deepening into class antipathy. . . .

"That systematic education would lead to greater equality in the distribution of wealth, to a truer appreciation of each man's worth, and to a deeper interest of each man in his neighbor's well-doing, is not difficult to recognize. First, by equality of education inequalities in birth and fortune are in some measure equalized. Second, when all men of the same district and of the same age have been trained up in the same technical schools, even though some have enjoyed a longer period there than others, it will follow that their talents and characters are known to and appreciated by their comrades; and the place of each man in the rank and file of society is felt and conceded. The fool cannot set up as master, nor the ignorant man as foreman; neither would it be permitted, that, without merit, one man should monopolize a large portion of the joint earnings. The master's merits will be valued on some such principle as the man's merits; and the share of the joint produce to which a master may be fairly entitled would be subject to the same appreciation as the earnings of each man. Capital would still be entitled to interest, and labor to wages; but why capital should absorb the profits of labor would be a question as open to debate as why one man should reap the crop which another had labored. In actual trade a very common practice is, that capital shall not merely have interest, but shall, in addition, put a large quantity of wages into the pocket of the capitalist, to which he gives the name of business profits; and that, of course, is so much subtracted from the wages of the men who do the work: but when education has given to each man a knowledge of all the branches of his work, and there remains no difference of rank, excepting superior skill and intelligence, then each man's individual work will be weighed in the balance; and the true share of his merit will be appraised in the scale of wages. The question will be, how much in that scale the true earnings of one man outweigh those of another. Under the present system, the master of a thousand men may pocket, in the shape of profits, one-half of the whole earnings of all the men, or he may pocket only a sum equal to the wages of a hundred men; but it will then be a matter for consideration whether one man in the same trade, possessing skill of the same sort, can really be entitled to a just charge for his services of ten or a hundred times the wages of his skilled and educated fellow. It is plain, that, under such a scale of estimation, these unequal proportions would be likely to diminish; and in the end that would be considered great merit which should give a man not only the honor of leading his fellow-craftsmen, but also the advantage of double wages: the idea of giving him tenfold or a hundred-fold would have disappeared from the catalogue of possibilities. The education of the future will, therefore, lead to a great reduction of masters' wages or profits, and to a fair, fixed remuneration for capital invested, and to a fair division of the earnings for work among those skilled men who execute it, in some recognized proportion to the contribution which their skill makes to the common work. Equality will be then, as now, impossible; but the scale of each man's life may be one of steady, continual, meritorious rise. . . .

"In our opinion, the philosophers are far before the people in foreseeing the times that are coming; and the people don't take warning because they are not educated. Agriculture is in revolution; for agriculture is becoming chemistry, and husbandry is becoming machinery: yet our agriculturists have not become chemists, nor our husbandmen mechanics. In common trades a revolution is coming; for all that is done without skill is going to be done by dead machinery, not by intelligent men; and it is well that it should be so, for mere routine processes, requiring brute strength, without refinement or intelligence, can all be better done, more evenly, regularly, and unvaryingly, by dead matter than by living force; and it is, moreover, better for the intelligent and moral being that he should not be degraded to the level of the brute elements, or lowered to the rank of an unsentient machine. Why should a human being be doomed to spend his days in mounting and descending a ladder with twenty-seven burnt bricks on his shoulder, while, at one-tenth of the cost, a machine made of iron, and fed with coal, will do the work, if he will only undertake the more intelligent task of tending, feeding, oiling, and repairing it? This last demands education, intelligence, conscientious care, all the qualities that go to make a man a superior, thoughtful being. Who, then, can regret the time coming when every occupation which requires no skill, and only brute force, shall cease to be the daily work of a human being, and when that being shall be raised to be a maker, worker, or director of machines?

"To that time the working-man is rapidly approaching, and for it he must be fitted; but above and over him will arise the class, who, in their turn, are to instruct, guide, and think for him. However skilled to work his machine, he will still depend on a superior to invent or make it; on a man who shall go before him to lay out his work and prepare it; on a man who shall come after him to complete it. These are the higher departments which form the higher ranks of crafts: in short, above the skilled doers we must have the skilled thinkers.

"In this view of an intelligent, skilled nation, it is plain that we shall be able to do without the unskilled, the unintelligent, and the uneducated. We shall not merely be able to do without him; but we shall think it better to be without him. The law of society will become this, — that he who cannot create his food shall not eat it; for assuredly in the time that is coming he will not find in civilized Europe a place for him. The man of the future must have one of two qualifications, — skill to do, education to know, — or both. . . .

"What is, then, the mercantile or moneyed value of a well-trained skilful Englishman, as compared to a strong, able-bodied man who understands no craft, handiwork, or art? The shop-value of the two men is at once told by the labor-market. The one man can earn for the community twenty-five pounds a year; the other man has an average of sixty pounds, and, with superior skill, a hundred pounds a year. Or if we take the three grades of unskilled, moderately skilled, and highly skilled men, we may represent their mean values by twenty-five pounds, fifty pounds, and seventy-five pounds: in other words, the highly skilled man is worth three times the value of the unskilled man.

"At the present time, there are (in England) about a million of skilled workmen; but there are a million of very poorly skilled, and two millions of utterly unskilled men. Supposing that by education we can raise the million of lower skilled into highly skilled men, and replace them by one million of unskilled men, raised by some little education to their rank, we have by that single act earned for the country fifty million pounds a year.

"We can now put the question in a new and very precise form: Is the addition of fifty million pounds per annum to the nation's wealth, through increased training, knowledge, and skill, worth the annual outlay of a million pounds from the nation's budget.

"There is, however, an important practical question to be asked. Skill, capacity, and ability are not in themselves wealth; and it may not be clear and obvious how this additional fifty million pounds is to be earned without the addition of a single man to the population. The manner in which skill creates wealth is not difficult to understand. Take one million tons of the iron which we export from this country in little better than the brute form in which Nature has providently stored it up for us immediately below the skin of our soil, and for which we now receive barely three million pounds; let us suppose that we expend upon that iron a little of the skill which Mr. Bessemer, the great technical schoolmaster in steel, can so readily teach us; and let us convert it into, say, half a million of Bessemer steel rails, and it will at once have risen to the value of six million pounds: the other half million of tons have gone to supply the waste, and pay the other costs of the process. In this case skill has earned three million pounds sterling in a highly marketable commodity. But we need not stop here. The steel in these rails may be converted by still higher skill into boilers, wheels, axles, and parts of locomotive engines; and, if the skilled workmen of our country are more skilled than those elsewhere, a hundred thousand tons of that steel may be worked up into two thousand locomotive engines and tenders, which will alone be worth four million pounds; and thus the value of this portion of the steel is quadrupled.

"It is easy to imagine what may be done with the remaining four hundred thousand tons of steel. Part of it might be converted into agricultural steam-engines and steam-ploughs to till every man's fields; and in that shape the value of each ton might be taken at fifty pounds a ton; so that a hundred thousand tons would become worth five million pounds. Another portion might form the steel of still smaller tools and implements, which, in proportion to their smallness and the higher ratio of skill and artifice, would easily become of double the value, or ten million pounds. There can hence be no difficulty in seeing how the higher skill of the additional million of skilled men whom we have raised by education could be able to earn their twenty-five additional millions of higher wages; and, moreover, there can be no difficulty in seeing how the less skilled million below them could earn their additional wages as helpers to these, or as users and employers of the improved tools and machinery which the others had created. . . .

"But to return to the mere vulgar usefulness of educated human beings. I will venture a remark from personal experience in my profession, which I trust may illustrate the vast importance to us of educating not only governors, or masters, but of extending a high scientific education and skilled technical training to the working-men of all skilled occupations. It is this: The community at large are deprived of the use of enormous treasures in mechanical invention, and enormous progress in scientific arts, by the fact of the general want of education in those who practise them. It may not be known, but it is yet true, that the mechanical power employed in all our manufactures is infinitely more costly than it need be. It is equally true that some skilled men of such professions know thoroughly how to produce immense economy in the production and use of mechanical power; but that we dare not put the means into the hands of the uneducated masters under whose control they would be applied. I am not now speaking of a loss of five, ten, twenty, or thirty per cent: I say that we know that *we are only utilizing one-tenth to one-twentieth of the power we employ and waste, and that an economy of one hundred, two hundred, three hundred, and four hundred per cent, is quite within our power so soon as a better informed, higher skilled, more perfectly trained class of men and masters shall arise,* who are fit to be trusted with the use of instruments and tools at present utterly beyond their comprehension, control, or application to use."

The following is from the Nineteenth Report (made in 1872) of the Science and Art Department of the Committee of Council of Education, England: —

"The steam class established by Mr. Taylor, Cushnie, Kincardineshire, for the instruction of ploughmen in the management of agricultural steam-machinery, has also been successful. Mr. Taylor writes, 'As to the ploughmen's class in steam and mechanics, there is no doubt, that, after draining, cultivation by steam-power is one of the greatest modern improvements in agriculture; but the great want is skilled men in the different districts competent to work the engines. The class has done much good in dispelling prejudice which existed among ploughmen against steam-cultivation and evening classes. For the first time they find that education has a money-value. In the last letter I had from one of the men sent to the Scottish Steam-Cultivation Company, he told me he was then earning twenty-five shillings a week: when he left, about six months ago, his wages would be about fourteen shillings. All the others I have sent are getting not less than nineteen shillings.' In a subsequent letter, Mr. Taylor states that he has received an application for twenty additional trained ploughmen, — an application he is unable to comply with. The demand for skilled labor of this description is so great, that Mr. Taylor intends carrying out his class through the summer months, instead of, as customary, only in the winter."

10*

CHAPTER III.

IMPORTANCE OF VARIED EDUCATION.

THE testimony of the extracts given in this chapter seems to place it beyond question, that, —

1. Special knowledge is not sufficient to produce even the best special results. The best workman is always the one who has a knowledge of tools and principles beyond the direct requirement of his work, whatever that may be. The best scientist is always the one who acquaints himself with other departments of science than the one to which he is specially devoted. The best artist is always the one who does not limit himself to his specialty, but studies the whole circle of art. This breadth of study and work gives a breadth of knowledge and training which decidedly strengthens the man for his specialty, be that however rude.

2. A thorough technical education, embracing all that science and art can bestow, is not enough to produce the best industrial results: there is need of the addi-

tional discipline which comes only from the study of letters. The man must be *formed*, as well as *informed*, before he is fully educated even for practical purposes. In science and art alone there is not enough of the formative, disciplining, shaping element. Whether they have more of this element or less than letters, may be a debatable question; but they certainly have less than science, art, and letters together. Hence, in the education of workmen, the literary and the technical should combine; the more of each, the better.

3. Since apprenticeship has virtually ceased through the subdivision of labor, it is doubly necessary that the public schools should give the elements, scientific and artistic, which form the basis of a technical education. And they should do this without diminishing the literary culture they now impart. Only by such an enlargement of the common school curriculum can the great body of laborers secure the education so essential for their welfare, and be kept from degenerating into mere machines for doing a limited variety of work.

4. The introduction of systematic manual labor into public schools for elementary instruction appears to be a thing of altogether doubtful expediency. Girls may be advantageously taught the use of the needle; while boys may, by way of pastime, be taught the use of a few tools by using them. In technical schools, how-

ever, manual labor may be judiciously introduced; but it should never take the leading place. This manual labor should always be of such a character as to show the student the practical application of his studies, and not labor simply to aid the student in supporting himself. It is questioned by some whether there should be any manual labor at all in the highest technical schools; they preferring that the student should acquire what of practical application he needs by work in actual fields of labor. But in apprentice schools, — schools attached to workshops and manufactories, — as it is the leading object of these schools to teach practical applications, systematic manual labor should, of course, form the leading feature of the instruction given. There can be no doubt that a certain amount of manual labor, especially if it shows the practical application of the theory which the student is acquiring, does not retard, but decidedly promotes, his progress in theoretical knowledge.

LITERARY AND SCIENTIFIC TRAINING.

The following is from the evidence of M. Monjean, Director of the Chaptal Municipal School, Paris, taken by the French Imperial Commission mentioned in the last chapter: —

"M. Monjean's observations on the results of the practical schools (*Real Schulen*) in Germany have led him to the conclusion, that the prevalence of an instruction purely practical, and based entirely on the applied sciences, has directed the attention of young men exclusively to subjects of self-interest and immediate profit, and has quenched the generous aspiration which sees in life something else than mere profit to be realized: the moral, in fact, is sacrificed to the mechanical man. Moreover, though the German practical schools have produced such moral results, they have not obtained for industry and commerce the objects they had in view. On this point, practical experience has given decisive evidence. Some merchants of Cologne and of Magdeburg, having selected from the practical schools and the gymnasia a certain number of young men of equal intelligence and capabilities, placed them at the same kind of work. For a short time, the pupils who had been brought up at the former schools maintained a certain degree of superiority; but, when they had been submitted to a longer period of probation, it was found that they were beaten by the pupils of the gymnasia, who, having received a more general and intelligent education, were better adapted for all pursuits to which they might be called."

These extracts are from the evidence of M. Pompée, founder and proprietor of the professional school at Ivry, vice-president of the Polytechnic Society, &c., taken by the French Imperial Commission: —

"M. Pompée finds the results of the instruction, and the success of his pupils, to be most satisfactory. The methods adopted are of a character to keep the attention always on the stretch; and boys whom want of success in their classical studies has rendered dull, apathetic, and idle, have recovered at the Ivry school all their activity of mind: their reasoning powers are awakened; they take an interest in their work; masters have not to punish, nor parents to complain. The employers under whom they find situations on leaving school are the first to discover the great difference between pupils trained on this plan and those who have received a classical education.

"On the whole, M. Pompée thinks that the tendency to attend special rather than general instruction is rapidly increasing in France, notwithstanding its present incomplete organization. Even in the university, the inspectors-general have had occasion to remark the constant augmentation in the number of those who attend the special classes. . . .

"In reply to the question as to what should be done to organize in France a complete system of professional education, M. Pompée advocates changes of rather a sweeping character. He likens his plan to a railway system, with its main-line stations, junctions, and branch lines. First, taking all the courses of study at present pursued at the primary schools, the technical schools, the communal colleges, and the lycées, he would from them construct one general course, to extend over nine years, and to be pursued by all alike, rich or poor, upper, middle, or lower class, sitting side by side on the same benches. This would form the main line of his system; but it would be impossible for all to reach the advanced years of the course. Just as passengers on a railway get out at the different stations, so the children, who, from pecuniary necessity or social position, are compelled to earn their livelihood at an earlier age, might leave school at any point of this course, subject to certain conditions. Along the main line he would place his branch lines, — the special schools, which would take at particular periods from the general course those children who have to adopt a distinct career in life. Thus all the passengers would be admitted indiscriminately to the same train: they can book themselves for any destination, they can be carried to the end of the journey, or be set down at any station they may please. If they have been put down at any station, and have changed their mind as to their destination, they can continue on the same road, or rejoin the nearest branch, without being obliged to retrace their steps. In other words, if such a general and uniform course of study were adopted, we should see at the end of every scholastic year pupils, more or less advanced, leaving the various classes, all, according to the amount of knowledge they have acquired, able to take their proper place in the different strata of social stratification,—some entering at once the factory, the counting-house, or the workshop; others to undergo their apprenticeship in the agricultural, commercial, industrial, or art schools which are ready to receive them.

"As regards the principal course, the subjects of instruction would be arranged progressively for each succeeding year of the nine years over which it would extend; but they would be taught in a different order, and on different methods from those now adopted. Thus, M. Pompée would postpone the commencement of the study of the ancient languages (of use only to the minority) until the pupil has reached an advanced class, when, by reason of the knowledge he has already acquired, and by the development of his faculties, he could in four years complete with pleasure and interest the classical studies which now occupy the whole of his time, and leave behind them often nothing but the recollection of fatigue and annoyance. At this time, that is to say, when the pupil is thirteen or fourteen years of age, the others who had not determined to study Latin or Greek will either have left school altogether, or have been drafted into the institutions for special instruction. By this means, all will have received a thoroughly sound elementary and general education, forming a foundation for the superstructure of an extended professional or technical training."

In their special report on Bavaria, the Sub-Commission of the French Imperial Commission says: —

"The system of industrial education adopted in 1864 has recently undergone important modifications, which have been suggested by experience, and are well deserving of attention. In the order of things established in virtue of a new law, which was passed after long discussions, the trade schools were to draw one part of their pupils from those educated in the primary schools, and the other from those of the Latin schools, which have four classes: the pupils from the latter, however, were to begin with the second year's course of studies. On the other hand, the instruction given in the trade schools, which have been somewhat ambitiously called *scientific gymnasia*, was of an order high enough to enable those who had received it entire to enter the polytechnic institutes.

"But the difference in the origin and preparation of the pupils of these schools opposed a serious obstacle to the progress of the teaching; and it was likewise ascertained, that, if the pupils who entered polytechnic institutes from the literary gymnasia appeared at first inferior to the others for scientific studies, they generally, at a later period, attained the superiority over those from the scientific gymnasia. The pupils from these last-named establishments were also open to the reproach of not possessing sufficient literary instruction, of being unable to express their thoughts in a clear and elegant style, and of being commonplace both in thought and language. Five years since, the Bavarian Council of Bridges and Roads had decided on admitting into the body of government engineers none but those, who, before entering the Polytechnic School, had followed the complete course of the literary gymnasia. The Administration of Mines had also constantly required the same qualifications.

"One of the distinguished men, who, for many years past, have studied this important question, has explained the change which had come over his ideas on this matter. Being a devoted friend and successful cultivator of the sciences, he was persuaded that their study, the habit of following their methods of explaining and of applying their results, was calculated, as well as the culture of letters, to develop the intelligence, and form the habit of clearly expressing thought in good language, at the same time that it was capable of giving a higher tone to mind. While professing chemistry, physics, and natural history in one of the first trade schools of the kingdom, he had strenuously supported this opinion, which greatly contributed to procuring him the appointment of professor in the Munich Polytechnic Institute, still retaining his chair in the trade school. In the first-named establishment he had to deal with pupils from the trade school or scientific gymnasium, and also with those from the literary gymnasium. But he soon made the discovery, that, though the pupils trained to scientific studies appear at first most competent to follow out their applications, those who come from the literary gymnasia, after completing their studies there, were not long ere they surpassed the others. This personal experience, after long and conscientious observation, won over this eminent professor to the opinion that the culture of letters gives the mind a clearness of conception and expression most favorable to the study of the sciences.

"The experience of the military schools at Metz and Saint-Cyr in France has long since shown that the pupils who have been so fortunate as to combine advanced literary acquirements with the study of the sciences are nearly always those who attain most distinction in after-life.

"The result of the criticism and discussion to which the old system gave rise is embodied in the new system, which makes the trade schools (*Gewerbe Schulen*) a continuation of the primary schools, to prepare pupils for the schools of agriculture, commerce, and ordinary industry. By the side of the literary gymnasia for classical studies, there are now practical gymnasia (*Real Gymnasien*), which impart a literary and scientific instruction sufficient for pupils who intend to enter the polytechnic institutes. This system is almost identical with that adopted in France in 1852, chiefly with a view to the literary instruction of youth destined for the public services, with this fundamental and advantageous difference, however, that, in Bavaria, the two kinds of establishments are separated instead of being united.

"Under the present system, the establishments for technical education are divided into, —

"1. Industrial or trade schools (*Gewerbe Schulen*), to which, according to local requirements, may be annexed special divisions for commerce, agriculture, &c.

"2. Practical gymnasia.

"3. A polytechnic school, comprising four special divisions, — for constructions, technical mechanics, technical chemistry, and commerce."

Mr. Samuelson says, in the letter quoted from in the last chapter: —

"I was told by several competent observers, that, although the *Real Schule* or the *Gewerbe Schule* may be a more preferable introduction to the factory and the merchant's office than the gymnasium (and even this is denied by some), the superior mental training of the gymnasium far more than compensates for the greater amount of 'knowledge' supposed to be acquired in the former as a preparation for the polytechnic school; and this applies even in a greater degree to the *Gewerbe Schule,* in which the technical instruction is more special, than to the *Real Schule,* where it is more general. However this may be, and it affords matter for reflection, in the organization of our own public schools, it is certain that the neglect of literary instruction in the *Gewerbe Schulen,* as now organized, tends to deprive their pupils of the breadth of cultivation which is the distinctive characteristic of the Germans."

The *École Centrale des Arts et Manufactures,* France, is probably the most celebrated school of the applied sciences in the world. From the two thousand young men who have left this school have come many of the most distinguished manufacturers and engineers. In their first prospectus the founders of this school said, "All the subjects really form only one and the same course: industrial science is one. Every one engaged in any branch should possess it in its entirety, under pain of inferiority to the competitor who is better armed in the struggle than himself."

MANUAL LABOR.

The following extract is from the evidence of M.

Marguerin, director of the Turgot Municipal School, Paris, taken by the French Imperial Commission: —

"M. Marguerin is not of opinion that the introduction of manual labor into technical schools would be productive of any practical benefit. He considers that one of the great advantages of the system of education established at the Turgot and other schools of the same description is, that the pupil has completed all his more important studies before he is too old to enter upon his apprenticeship. In order that the pupil might undergo a course of manual labor at school, he would be compelled to sacrifice some of the more important branches of general education, which the teacher finds to be so useful in the training of his pupils. It is a common argument to refer to the professional school at Mulhouse; but it must be borne in mind that the manual labor at that school is confined to two hours of joiners' work in the week, and that this labor is considered more as an athletic exercise than as a preparation for apprenticeship; also that the mechanical workshop, the chemical laboratory, the school of design, and the weaving workshop, which form a part of the Mulhouse school, only take in pupils after they have received several years of general instruction. . . .

"In summing up what he has to say upon the subject, M. Marguerin repeats his objections to the introduction of manual labor into schools. In the first place, he believes that the expense of providing teachers and tools for instruction in so many branches of trade and manufacture would form a serious consideration; secondly, that the schools are not likely to reap any profit from the sale of the manufactured article, as it can scarcely be supposed that in this they can compete with well-trained and skilled artisans."

M. Pompée, founder and proprietor of the professional school at Ivry, is reported as saying in his evidence before the French Imperial Commission: —

"For instruction in manual labor *time* is wanting: it is impossible to select from the subjects now taught any one which could be sacrificed to it. If, indeed, time could be found without injuring the training in elementary schools, what kind of manual labor should be chosen? Should it be the plane, the file, the chisel, or the shuttle? And where would be room for the bench, the lathe, the anvil, or the loom? Where can be found a master capable of teaching the use of these tools, and of many others? It is true, in case of necessity, the use of the spade and the rake might be introduced into rural schools; but at that age it could serve rather as an athletic exercise than as a profitable training. It would be far better to devote the time to the acquirement of the elements of natural science, chemistry, or mechanics, which, as agriculturists, the children could apply in after-life. Of course, the use of the needle should not be neglected in girls' schools, because, whatever their position, all women should become seamstresses for their own families. Another strong objection to the introduction of manual labor into schools would be its great cost; the necessary enlargement of the school, the tools and machines (to be renewed with every improvement), the raw material (for which, when unskilfully manufactured, there would be no sale), would be sources of enormous expense. In one word, M. Pompée sums up, manual labor out of the workshop is nothing but a pastime."

In the examination of Messrs. Gaumont and Guemied, editors of "The Journal of Professional Education," by the French Imperial Commission, they said: —

"It is often objected, that, by reason of the great varieties of operations in manual labor, it would be hopeless to find an individual endowed with an aptitude or sufficient flexibility of the organs to learn them all. But, according to the ideas of M. Gaumont and the gentlemen who think with him, the processes of all manufacturing industries can be reduced to a certain small number of identical manual operations. Thus the processes and tools employed in working in metals have many analogies with those used in working in wood: for example, whether a workman turns in metal or in wood; whether he turns by the aid of the bow, of the foot, or of a machine moved by steam-power, — the operation reduces itself to nearly the same method of manipulation. So in fitting, it always depends on a correct eye and manual skill; and the individual who can fit a piece of iron by means of the file will soon fit a piece of wood with the aid of plane and chisel. Thus both in technical and apprentice schools can be taught the fundamental manual operations which are employed in all manufactures. Turning and fitting would form the practical portion of the instruction, geometry and linear drawing the theoretical part, and the elements of general technology the higher and finishing part.

"If we consider manual labor merely as a means of instruction, it will still find a place in the technical school. A knowledge of manipulation is required in the chemical art: why should it be otherwise in a knowledge of the construction of machines and buildings? It is only possible to teach by four methods: 1st, Oral explanation given by the teacher; 2d, Written explanation taken from books; 3d, Graphic explanation rendered by drawing; and, 4th, Practical explanation obtained from execution. Up to the present time, only the first three methods of demonstration have been employed, and nothing but theorists produced: the moment that it is desired to train practical men, the fourth method will be added, and technical instruction will have been founded. Every technical school must admit into its course the manual labor of the workshop and of the laboratory: that is its distinctive characteristic, the cause of its existence. This principle admitted on general grounds, it becomes still more incontestable when applied to special industries. Machine manufacture, building, dyeing, weaving, &c., require not only a knowledge of applied science, but also a practical acquaintance with manual operations. Thus, by the side of industrial schools with general programmes, there must exist special schools for particular trades, established, like the first, to train managers and foremen; then, for a lower class, apprentice schools, and public courses of lectures for workmen, whether apprentices or adults."

The French Commission report M. Maignen, director of a Mission for the Succor of Apprentices, as saying: —

"With regard to school workshops, M. Maignen does not think that they are productive of benefit. An apprentice can only become a good workman by seeing others at work, and by learning the large processes of manufacture. It is in the motion and life of a large undertaking that the intelligence and ability of a young man develops itself, that he comprehends the value of a particular material, that he learns the manner in which, and the conditions under which, it can be best worked. On the contrary, the young man in a small school workshop is at no pains to be industrious, and never acquires any great degree of skill."

M. Bernat, Director of the School of Industrial Arts

and Mines at Lille, testifies before the same Commission:—

"The training given in the workshops is intended to accustom the pupils to the working of machines and looms, to give them manual skill, a practical acquaintance with the processes of execution, a knowledge of the difficulties which the raw material opposes to mechanical action, and, finally, to fit them specially for undertaking the charge of workshops and the direction of workmen. By this means, the works executed excite their emulation, and the action of the machines becomes familiar to them; the whole forming a technical and experimental system of instruction which could be replaced by no other."

In his evidence before the French Commission, M. Rossat, Doctor of Science, head master at Charleville, is reported thus:—

"Altogether, M. Rossat has observed that the practical are in no way injurious to the theoretical studies: on the contrary, in the subjects descriptive geometry and industrial drawing, manual labor seems to stimulate the pupils. Practical work in the shops and laboratory occupies two hours a day; and yet the pupils beg that that time may be extended. Already many of them possess great skill. The shops and all the works are under the direction of a civil engineer; and under him are three foremen,—one in the fitting, another in the smith's, and the third in the carpenter's shop. The proceeds of the labor of the pupils, if any, goes towards the maintenance of the workshops. In the fitting-shop, the most skilful pupils are at present occupied in putting together a steam-engine to replace the portable engine which now drives the machinery: others are making models and parts of machines to be placed in the machinery collection of the museum. The carpenters, of whom there are about thirty, learn the use of the saw, the plane, and the lathe: they make patterns for the iron casters, joiners' work, and carpenters' work, and models for solid geometry. There are fifty smiths engaged at the forge in the repair of tools, &c.; and in the same shop there are employed a few pupils who are intended for the veterinary schools. Lastly, under the direction of the head master himself, the remaining pupils are occupied with manipulations in the laboratory."

In his evidence before the French Commission, M. Malet, Professor at the Imperial Artillery School at Douai, says: —

"Attached to the classes are two apprentice-workshops, — one for working in wood, the other for working in iron, each in charge of a director, who is engaged to give in it practical instruction in manual labor. These workshops are situated in an annex of the town hall, which contains the normal school, and the upper primary school. The practice includes, in the one shop, working at the forge, fitting, and turning in metals; in the other, joining, carpentry, upholstery, and turning in wood. It is expected, that, in time, these shops will be capable of turning out work which can be sold, and become a source of profit to the institution. The number of pupils is nearly fifty, about equally divided between the shops. Work is carried on every day, except Thursday and Sunday: it begins at half-past five, and concludes at half-past eight, in the morning."

In their account of the Central Imperial School of

Arts and Manufactures, the French Commission say: —

"It has been said that the pupils of the school ought to devote a part of their time, like those of the schools of arts and trades, to manual operations; that they would then become far more capable of managing workshops. It is a mistake to think that intellectual and manual labor can be combined without inconvenience. Experience has proved that they injure each other. It is not absolutely necessary to be able to perform every manual operation one's self in order to see that artisans do their work properly; and it has often been found that he who pays excessive attention to details neglects the general effect. Should it, however, be deemed necessary to initiate a young man in the operations of the workman, let him, on leaving the school, pass a year or two in a good workshop, executing all kinds of work; and he will thus learn far better than by practising at school."

In their report giving the conclusions at which they had arrived from the evidence taken, the French Commission say: —

"In general, the reproach brought against every school-workshop is, that it does not realize the necessary industrial advantages; and especially that it does not accustom the pupils to that rapidity of execution which is one of the principal conditions of economical production. These objections are serious ones; and most of the examples on which they are founded do but too well justify them."

CHAPTER IV.

SPECIAL SCHOOLS FOR THE INSTRUCTION OF APPRENTICES.

WITH the decay of apprenticeship, numerous special schools for the instruction of apprentices have been established in Europe. These schools are supported in part by local, and in part by State contributions. The service they have rendered to industry cannot be lightly estimated.

Such schools can have no uniform organization, since they must be adapted to the industrial wants of each locality. One will be a school for weaving, another for lace-making, another for dyeing, another for watch-making, another for jewellers, another for machinists, another for carpenters, another for ship-builders, and so through the catalogue of industries. Of course, those things which are common to different industries can be taught in the same school.

Labor performed under the direction of experienced workmen occupies a good part of the time: the remainder is given to those studies which have an immediate bearing upon the industry taught. It is drawing, that, in nearly all of these schools, holds the leading place. When the early education has been sadly neglected, general instruction is sometimes given. Not only can the apprentice be taught more quickly and much better in one of these schools than he can be taught in the workshop, under the present system of labor, but he can be taught much more cheaply. As a general rule, a "green hand" is not regarded as a valuable acquisition to any industrial establishment. Even for such simple work as weaving cotton cloth, there is a perpetual contest among the cotton manufacturers of New England to secure operatives of experience. Indeed, some mills refuse to employ a "green hand" under any circumstances, considering it cheaper, as well as much less vexatious, to employ those only who have have had experience, though obliged to pay them more for the same yards woven. There can be no doubt that it is quite time apprentice-schools were established at all the manufacturing centres of the country, in imitation of those in Europe.

Reference has already been made to the reports of the British artisans sent to the World's Exhibition at Paris. Some of these artisans visited other parts of France. John Gregory and James Stringer, watchmakers, thus describe: —

MUNICIPAL SCHOOL OF THEORETICAL AND PRACTICAL WATCH-MANUFACTURE AT BESANÇON.

"This school is founded to secure the professional education of young people who intend devoting themselves to the art of watch-making. The city of Besançon is the principal seat of the manufacture of watches in France. The manufacturers of this city, almost exclusively supply the French market, as, of 378,498 watches sold in France in 1865, Besançon supplied 296,012, or nearly four-fifths of the whole number.

"The school has for its object thoroughly to teach children the trade they intend to follow; to supply, in fact, the notorious deficiencies of an actual apprenticeship: and, if the apprentices at the present time are so ignorant of the practical part of their trade, they are much more so of the theoretical part. The object this school is now carrying out on a large scale is to offer to young watchmakers an opportunity of constant comparison of the theory of watchmaking with the results at which they arrive practically.

"The regular time for this practical and theoretical course is three years; but it is desirable that the students whose aptitude and conduct is reported favorably of should prolong their stay at the school, in order to perfect themselves. The classes are held in a large building belonging to the city, the situation of which is all that could be desired. The classes are under the management of a director, who carefully sees that each branch of study is diligently followed out. The teaching is divided in the following manner:—

First Year.—(Third Division.)

"*Practical Teaching.*—Filing, turning, hardening, and tempering metal, perfecting small tools for doing first halves of the ordinary sizes.

"*Theoretical Teaching.* — Revision of early education, arithmetic, mensuration, geography, mechanical drawing, general principles, making the more simple tools and machines employed in watch-making.

Second Year. — (*Second Division.*)

"*Practical Teaching.* — Doing first halves of various sizes, pivoting, and making the different parts of a cylinder escapement.

"*Theoretical Teaching.* — Studying style, geography, arithmetic, elementary geometry and its application, mechanical drawing, geometrical models, models of tools and machines used in watchmaking, designs of the different parts of a watch.

Third Year. — (*First Division.*)

"*Practical Teaching.* — Constructing and planting the escapement, examining, regulating.

"*Theoretical Teaching.* — Course of mechanics, ideas of industrial chemistry, cosmography, commercial book-keeping and general geography, mechanical drawing, study of various cut-wheels, models of escapements, and designing watch-movements for the model.

"The theoretical lectures are given in each division every day, from seven to nine o'clock in the morning, Thursday excepted.

"The work-hours are from nine o'clock in the morning till noon, and from half-past one till five.

"Drawing-lessons are given in each division on Mondays, Tuesdays, and Fridays, from five till seven o'clock in the evening.

"The course of commercial book-keeping and general geography for the first division is held every Wednesday, from five to seven in the evening.

"On Saturday, the director examines the pupils in the work of the week, so as to note step by step the progress made. In addition to the instruction given in the school, the pupils are taken from time to time to the different manufactories in the neighborhood, so that they may become familiarized with the various combinations and applications of machinery; and also to different workshops where the several parts of a watch are made. The knowledge which they thus acquire of the methods used in the actual process of manufacture, and which can only be gained in the workshops themselves, completes the education indispensable to a thorough knowledge of watchmaking.

"The school is visited each week by two members of the Board of Directors composed of the most skilled men in the trade, who take note of the quality of the work done, as well as of the progress of the pupils. At the expiration of each scholastic year, the pupils are subjected to a general examination, at the end of which prizes are awarded to the most deserving pupils. The distribution of these prizes takes place in public, under the direction of the mayor.

"This distribution is preceded and followed by a public exhibition of the productions of the manual labor of the students, and the designs executed by them, during the year. The vacation begins on the first of September, and continues during that month.

"The conditions of admission into the school are as follows: —

"The school for watchmaking receives any young people, without distinction as to country or nationality. To be received into the school, the pupils must be able to read and write fluently, and know the four rules of arithmetic. They are examined before a special jury before being admitted."

The French Imperial Commission, which is more fully described in the second chapter, speak thus of apprentice-schools in Belgium: —

APPRENTICE SCHOOLS IN BELGIUM.

"Belgium offers in Western Flanders, by her communal schools for apprentice-weavers (*écoles communales d'apprentissage*), a remarkable example of the results that may be obtained in such institutions. These schools, in which primary and religious instruction is united with manual labor, are intended for the children of poor parents, and are adapted to the industry of the neighborhood; namely, weaving. The communes, aided by the State, have provided a building with looms; and, under the direction of a paid overseer, these school-shops work up raw material furnished by manufacturers of the neighborhood. The apprentices receive small wages, which increase with their capacity, until they know their trade well enough to be admitted into the factories, where they can earn a living. From fifty-five to sixty apprentice-schools of this kind are distributed over as many communes, and receive from thirteen thousand to fourteen thousand pupils. The official reports published at Bruges in 1863 show that everywhere instruction and habits of regular employment have produced the most successful results in improving the morals not only of the children, but also of the parents, and that mendicity and vagrancy have almost entirely disappeared from those districts.

"When the first attempts were made to organize apprentice-schools for the different sorts of manufactures, the exclusive and almost absolute direction was confided to masters who had an interest in them. It was, however, soon discovered that the authority charged with watching over the execution of the indentures on behalf of the children had not sufficient powers: consequently the majority of the institutions of that kind were allowed to die out; and in their place were substituted communal workshops, 'created exclusively for the professional instruction of the working-classes and in the general interest of trade; the committees of which endeavor to vary the instruction of the pupil as far as possible.

"'The pupils of those workshops are usually compelled to attend school for two hours; and, while the apprentice thus derives a rest by this cessation from labor, he at the same time acquires knowledge admitting of a general application. Experience has proved that the introduction of literary and moral instruction is effected with the greatest facility in those communal workshops in which it was not practised, and that it produces an excellent effect on the character and morals of the young workmen.

"'It has even been found that with the space of time devoted daily to instruction in reading, writing, the rudiments of arithmetic, &c., the pupils who attend the workshops learn almost as rapidly as those who are obliged to remain all the day at school.'

"This remark agrees with the observations made in England on the half-time schools. The object of these workshops not being merely to show the child a loom which is to enable him to gain a livelihood, but also to contribute to his intellectual and industrial progress, 'it is sought to instruct the pupils not only in weaving, properly so called, but also in the preparation of the warp, in arranging the loom for the execution of different patterns, in deciphering designs, and, in short, every thing belonging to the weaver's art.'

"In 1863, out of fifty-four apprentice-workshops established, in forty primary instruction was being given to the extent desired; and in fourteen only was it not completely organized. According to the official returns, the organization of those special apprentice-workshops, which only date from 1851, are at present fifty-four in number, comprising: —

Looms	1,285
Apprentice Pupils	1,652

"The number of workmen they have trained during a period of twelve years amounts to 13,481, the greater part rescued from want, mendicity, and all the vices they engender.

"Let us add in conclusion, as is remarked by the author of the report, M. Renier, inspector of the apprentice-workshops, that a number of young apprentices who had never entered a school have left the workshops with a fair knowledge of reading and writing; and that this important result has been obtained in the greater part of the communes which contain a workshop. It evidently results, from this observation, that the workshop, far from taking boys from the schools, is, with the aid of a good organization, a powerful means of extending the benefits of instruction, and of counteracting the selfish and short-sighted conduct of parents, who, without concerning themselves for the future, only think of the trifling salary to be earned promptly by an ignorant workman."

The French Imperial Commission thus speak of the power-loom weaving-school at Mulhouse: —

POWER-LOOM-WEAVING-SCHOOL AT MULHOUSE.

"The apprentice-workshops are not only of use in forming simple workmen: they may also constitute a sort of technical and special schools for preparing educated youths for the direction of manufactories. With this view, some manufacturers of Mulhouse, convinced of the utility of a complete instruction in the principles which should guide the manufacturer of the great variety of stuffs now produced, and enlightened by the example of Germany, raised by subscription, in 1861, a fund of thirty-seven thousand francs destined to found, as an experiment, a school of weaving with power-loom. This school, which is placed under the direction of M. E. Friès, admits thirty or forty out-door pupils, who pay a certain sum yearly, and receive a theoretical and practical instruction in the process of weaving, sufficient to enable them to superintend manufactories.

"To show in what degree such institutions meet the requirements of trade, it will not be without interest to exhibit the progressive results of the administration of that school during the first three years of its existence: —

Receipts and Expenditures of the School of Weaving at Mulhouse from Nov. 1, 1861, to Nov. 1, 1864.

Receipts of the School.		Expenses of the School.		Capital raised in 1861, by subscription, among the principal manufacturers and merchants of the Departments of the Haut-Rhin and Vosges, 37,000 francs.	
	Frs. C.		Frs. C.		Frs. C.
From Nov. 1, 1861, to Nov. 1, 1862,	6,178 10	From Nov. 1, 1861, to Nov. 1, 1862, current expenses.	14,000 80	Year 1861-1862. Drawn from the capital,	15,432 70
		Fitting up schoolrooms,	4,600 00		
		Purchase of machinery,	3,010 00		
		Total expenditure, 1861-1862,	21,610 80		
From Nov. 1, 1862, to Nov. 1, 1863.	12,540 50	From Nov. 1, 1862, to Nov. 1, 1863, current expenses,	12,721 05	Year 1862-1863. Drawn from the capital,	13,306 55
		Purchase of a steam-engine,	13,126 00		
		Total expenses in 1862-1863,	25,847 05		
From Nov. 1, 1863, to Nov. 1, 1864,	16,205 45	From Nov. 1, 1863, to Nov. 1, 1864, current expenses,	12,325 75	Year 1863-1864; excess of receipts over expenditure,	3,879 70

"The above table shows, that, after scarcely three years' existence and experience, this school, in which the number of pupils was at first only ten or twelve at the most, has been able to organize itself, purchase its material and a steam-engine; and yet, having borrowed for that purpose only 28,739 francs from the subscription-fund, it has obtained a net profit (its material and all expenses being paid) of 3,879 francs at the end of the third year. This result, which proves what benefit the manufacturing towns derive from making a judicious outlay for the promotion of technical instruction, determined the founders to give to their school of weaving a definite constitution, and to form, with that object, a company with a capital of seventy-six thousand francs, divided into seventy-six shares of a thousand francs each, which were subscribed for immediately.

"At present the school is established in a building erected for the purpose: it is provided with a steam-engine, with every thing that is necessary for transmitting the motive-power, and twenty-four different looms, on which various stuffs may be manufactured. It works not only as a theoretical and practical school of weaving, but also as an ordinary factory, so as to cover by the sale of its productions a part of the outlay.

"Its financial position in the month of September, 1864, was as follows: —

	Frs. C.
Capital, seventy-six shares at a thousand francs	76,000 00
Funds disposable March 1, 1864, from the first subscription	8,260 75
Surplus of receipts over expenditure in 1863–1864	3,879 70
Capital disposable on March 1, 1864	88,140 45
EXPENDITURE.	
March 1, 1864, purchase of ground and costs	10,018 00
Sept. 1, 1864, building of workshops	56,000 00
Total expenditure	66,018 00
Balance	22,122 45
	88,140 45

"The school opened under these favorable conditions on the 3d of October, 1864.

"The studies are partly theoretical, and partly practical; the pupils passing alternately and regularly from the one to the other. The theoretical studies consist principally of the decomposition and analysis of all kinds of stuffs, especially those which concern the manufactures of Alsace. The course is terminated by mechanical drawing, the study of the internal arrangements of manufactories with plans and estimates, the calculating of the cost-price of manufactures, and book-keeping. The practical studies consist of the working of the looms, the fitting-up, regulating, adjusting, preservation, and repair of all the machinery, and, lastly, the weaving itself in all its operations by the pupils themselves, assisted by an experienced foreman.

"The charge of admission to the theoretical and practical course of studies is six hundred francs for the scholastic year of eleven months; but the pupil is at liberty to attend only one of the two courses. Foreigners are admitted as well as Frenchmen.

"These studies are terminated by examinations before a board of manufacturers and engineers, which delivers certificates of capacity to the successful candidates. At this examination the pupils have to submit to the board a general plan of the school, with its steam-engine and apparatus for the distribution of the motive-power, and with drawings of the different machines, and the complete plan of a manufactory.

"It will be seen by the above details that nothing is neglected in the studies of the pupils, so that those who have received certificates of capacity are at once competent to direct manufactories of various kinds. We must add, that the manufacturers who founded this school of weaving are precluded from participating in the profits the establishment may make, and that they have only a right to the legal interest on the money they have advanced, and its reimbursement on the breaking up of the association."

CHAPTER V.

INSTRUCTION OF WORKMEN.

In various ways it has been attempted, with a greater or less degree of success, to improve the technical education of workmen after they have become workmen.

1. For this purpose popular lectures have been found serviceable. They must, however, be specific, and not general: they must have a direct bearing on the employment of the workmen. If the lectures deal with their subjects in a general way, they may entertain and perhaps stimulate somewhat; but they will prove of little advantage to the workmen. While imparting positive knowledge, they must not neglect the reason of things, but set the workmen to thinking.

But the workmen must have had some elementary technical instruction, or they will not be able to comprehend the lectures; for the lectures, to be of the best, cannot deal in glittering generalities, but must employ technical terms, and must usually assume that the hearers are acquainted with certain elementary data. The workmen must also have had some elementary literary instruction: for it is essential that they should take notes of the lectures; otherwise the knowledge imparted by the lectures will, in the main, be soon forgotten.

These things have been found essential to the success of popular lectures for the technical instruction of workmen.

2. For such instruction, evening schools have also been found serviceable. The room in which such schools are held should be well warmed and well ventilated: it should be well lighted from above, and in such manner as to prevent all cross-lights. These are general requisites. The equipment of the room must vary somewhat according to the character of the instruction given. As drawing is usually the leading thing to be taught in such schools, precedence must usually be conceded to that in the equipment of the room.

It has been found by experience that men actually engaged in the business in which instruction is to be given, as foremen, for example, and practical draughtsmen, make excellent teachers for these evening schools. These teachers from the workshop know just what the workmen require in the way of practical application: they know the obstacles to be overcome in applying the theory, and just how to overcome them. Usually they cannot explain the theory so well as the professional teacher; but their intimate knowledge of the practical applications of the theory enables them much better to satisfy the workmen, who are always impatient of a long drill in theory before coming to direct applications, — a course that can be successfully pursued in an ordinary school. The very best teacher, however, for these schools for workmen, is the professional teacher, who, to his knowledge of the teacher's art and to his knowledge of the theory of the thing to be taught, has added a knowledge of the practical applications of the theory, which he may readily add by investigations in the workshop. Thus it will be seen that there seldom need be a lack of good teachers in any place where an evening technical school is required.

Workmen and apprentices should be taught together. The latter not having advanced far enough in their business to appreciate the value of the instruction, they are too much inclined to neglect it when taught by themselves. But the example of the men stimulates them to study. As a rule, all under the age of fifteen years should be excluded from these evening schools.

When the school is small, there cannot well be more than one class; and all must attend to the same study at the same time. When the school is large, then it can be divided into two or more classes for the pursuit of different studies, or of different parts of the same study.

The teacher may give his explanations to the class as a whole, requiring all the members to attend to the same thing at the same time. Further assistance may then be rendered to individual members who failed to comprehend the explanations when given to the whole class. This plan enables the teacher to do the most for the whole class in an allotted time; but, on the other hand, the more zealous and intelligent members are kept back somewhat.

Or the teacher may explain only general principles to the class as a whole; each member making a different application of these principles. In the applications the teacher can render individual assistance. This plan does not restrain the more zealous and intelligent, nor need it deprive the laggards of suitable instruction, if the teacher is active. It also permits instruction to be given at the same time in two or three different trades, when they have common foundation principles, as they may have, for example, in chemistry, geometry, drawing. Thus much of the instruction in drawing required by the carpenter, machinist, and cabinet-maker must be of the same general character.

Or the instruction may be all oral, illustrated by experiments or diagrams. This has two or three grave disadvantages. The stupid require repetition, and sometimes those who are not stupid require it; but frequently it cannot be had, as in the case of experiments, or from lack of time. The study of the subject cannot, therefore, be continued out of school. Again: it is often essential that notes be taken; but this many workmen cannot do from lack of elementary instruction.

The conclusion is, that judicious blending of oral instruction with use of a text-book is much the best thing. All book is out of the question. The book should contain the theory, with some practical applications; but most of the latter must be got outside of books, and should be selected with special reference to the wants of the workmen receiving instruction. With the book before him, the workman more readily understands the teacher; with the explanations of the teacher, he more readily understands the book, though the teacher may not always express himself as clearly as the book. The book can also be used out of school, which is a great advantage. If, however, the workman's elementary instruction has been neglected, he will find himself troubled to use even the plainest book understandingly. Aside from text-books, the school should have books for general reference.

Whatever general mode of teaching is followed, speedy application of the theory must be a part of it, otherwise the workmen will lose their interest. Indeed, theory and practical application must go together from the outset in the instruction of workmen. It is also the conclusion of European experience, that a small fee should be changed for the instruction in these schools.

3. Museums have also been found exceedingly serviceable for the technical education of workmen. Local museums must conform to the wants of the different localities where they are established. Thus, in its local museum, the dominant industry of each district should be specially represented. If, for example, it is the production of machinery, the workman should be able to find in the museum illustrations of just what he desires to learn about the application of power, and the making of machines. If it is the production of textile fabrics, all the best and latest achievements of the loom should be there exemplified for the benefit of the local manufacturer; and so on. In every museum, however, for the culture in taste and delight of all should be gathered beautiful objects illustrating the different departments of art.

With well-stored museums, easy of access at all times, the workman can use his eyes to the greatest advantage in perfecting his technical education. Through the eye is the readiest approach to the mind. Frequently a single glance of the eye will give the workman a clearer comprehension of a principle in mechanics than he could obtain from a long explanatory discourse, or from reading a book. Then it has been well said that "taste is the recollection of the beautiful." Whether this definition be true or not, certain it is, that for the cultivation of the taste, which is so valuable in nearly all industrial arts, there must be beautiful objects for frequent contemplation and study. This lacking, all other instruction fails to impart correct taste.

4. In several European countries Sunday schools for the technical instruction of workmen are numerous, and well attended.

POPULAR LECTURES.

In their report, the French Imperial Commission, more fully described in the second chapter, speak thus of popular lectures for the instruction of workmen: —

"It will be remembered, that in 1819 the first industrial courses of lectures were founded and organized in various towns of France by the zealous efforts of Baron Charles Dupin. Responding to an appeal, in which he eloquently invoked the memory of Gaspard Monge, many pupils of the Polytechnic School, chiefly officers of engineers and artillery in the towns where they were in garrison, engineers of the bridges and roads and of mines, placed themselves at the disposal of the municipal authorities to diffuse a knowledge of science among the industrial population of every class. Of all these educational undertakings, the best organized and the most successful was the institution founded by the town of Metz, with the aid of MM. Poncelet, Bergery, and Bardin. The first-named of these gentlemen, ardent in the propagation of science, then entered on the course which he has since followed with such distinction, and which led him to explain by the aid of the rudiments of elementary geometry most of the principles and delicate problems of mechanical science. To him belongs the honor of having shown that it is not so difficult as might be supposed to popularize, and bring within the grasp of ordinary capacities, the study all the propositions of industrial mechanics.

"Since M. Poncelet, others, following in his steps, have sought to extend the same mode of teaching in the public lectures of the Conservatory of Arts and Trades, and in those of the Polytechnic and Philotechnic Associations; and their efforts have been attended with results of immense value. The first-named of these associations instituted in 1830 popular lectures, which were, from the very beginning, exclusively intrusted to ex-pupils of the Polytechnic School. These lectures have since been established in every quarter of Paris; and in 1860 this same association founded in the amphitheatre of the School of Medicine isolated lectures, which, in their turn, called public attention to this particular mode of disseminating useful knowledge among the people.

"But it would be wrong to lose sight of the fact that public lectures, or merely oral teaching, even when accompanied by experiments made with the aid of good models and of applications to common questions, often leave on the memory and understanding of the auditors only evanescent impressions. This effect is still more certain when the audience, composed exclusively of apprentices and workmen, is only prepared for the instruction given by an imperfect elementary education, which has not prepared them for mental effort, whilst their professional habits unceasingly draw them towards practical and material results. The consequence has been, that notwithstanding all the talent and zeal of the professors of public lectures, whether in Paris or in the large towns of France, this mode of teaching, in so far as it is specially devoted to working-men, has not produced all the results its founders expected, although truth compels the acknowledgment that it has not been altogether fruitless. . . .

"Though, for the technical teaching of workmen disposed to devote part of their leisure to studies which may be useful to them, it has been thought proper to give the preference to regular classes over public or simply oral lectures, it does not follow that such lectures, or even occasional meetings, may not be really useful. There are, in fact, a great many scientific and technical questions which possess great interest, not only for the workmen themselves, but also for their masters, for young men, and, indeed, for a host of people who would not submit to a regular attendance at such classes as those of which the organization has just been described, and which require punctuality and practical application. On the other hand, certain special branches of science, though very desirable to be learned, do not always admit of regular teaching, nor of any considerable number of lessons. A person well versed in the theory and practice of some particular art might be disposed to give a few lectures on the subject he has mastered, but would not choose to give a course limited to workmen only. Giving public lectures and holding meetings, in such cases, cannot be otherwise than beneficial; and although they are not so effective for the technical instruction of workmen, properly so called, as regular classes opened expressly for them, the fact is none the less certain, that, by diffusing and popularizing science and experience among the public who attend them, much good will be done."

EVENING SCHOOLS.

In his evidence before the French Commission, the Rev. Father Baudine, assistant superior of the Christian Brothers' School, says: —

"The classes are divided into two divisions, — one, open from six to eight o'clock in the evening, for apprentices from thirteen to sixteen years old; the other, from eight to ten, for workmen of sixteen, and above. Every year the works of the pupils are exhibited in one of the amphitheatres of the Conservatory of Arts and Trades. Each work bears the name of the pupil, his age, the time of his apprenticeship, and the name and address of his master. A board, composed of manufacturers of good position, awards and distributes the prizes.

"In different quarters of Paris, local committees, composed of manufacturers and persons of good position, have been formed to visit the different schools weekly, and to bring masters and apprentices into communication."

In his evidence before the same Commission, M. Bardin, professor of industrial drawing to the communal schools of the city of Paris, says: —

"There does not appear to be any disadvantage in causing both workmen and apprentices to meet in the same class; for apprentices rarely understand the utility of application, and they are encouraged by the industrious workmen who frequent the classes. . . .

"If the workmen paid, however small the sum, they certainly would be more regular in their attendance at the drawing-classes than they are now; and the instruction would be regarded more earnestly by them: this is a fact which has been attested by experience. This system has, besides, numerous precedents. The workmen in their practical courses take upon themselves the expenses of the premises and lighting. The private schools, receiving subsidies from the town, have about three hundred and fifty pupils who pay: moreover, a great number of workmen who enter their names for the courses of the communal schools come with the intention of paying.

"The only objection that could be made is in favor of apprentices, because they earn nothing. This is true; but, for those whose families could not afford these expenses, the masters, who give a little money every week to the youths working for them, as a recompense, would willingly pay the monthly fee of the school (which might be as low as possible), and would also undertake to see that the apprentice profits by the advantages offered to him."

Messrs. Gaumont and Guemied, editors of "The Journal of Professional Education," said to the French Commission: —

"All pupils attending public courses of instruction should pay a small fee, to give them an interest in their work. Everywhere where a good system of public instruction is maintained, this plan is adopted. At Mulhouse nothing is gratuitous: it is the same in all the Swiss cantons. At Paris the most frequented courses of drawing are those at the municipal schools, where a fee of from two to three francs is exacted monthly. . . .

"To give special instruction to workmen, it is of much or even of more importance, that the teacher should possess a knowledge of the trade than of pure science. It is almost indispensable to have lived the life of the workshop in order to be able to elevate the mere handicraftsman from practice to theory."

In their report, the French Imperial Commission express themselves in this wise:—

"In towns of moderate size, where the number of pupils, and consequently of professors, will be rather limited, it will generally be found advisable to unite pupils of equal proficiency in one class: thus there will be no other divisions to introduce but those indicated by the degree of progress in study. But the case will be very different in large towns; and, whenever the number of pupils shall exceed forty or fifty, it will be necessary to form several classes. It will then be advantageous to place workmen of the same or similar trades under a common course of instruction, which may be more particularly adapted to their occupation.

"Though it is impossible to indicate in a general report all the divisions which the requirements of local industries may thus introduce into technical education, still there are certain trades in which many workmen are engaged whose co-operation is indispensable to all the others, and for which it is possible to indicate the method in which the work to be executed by the pupils in their classes ought to be conducted. Among these industries, that of building is at once the most general, and also comprises the largest number of different trades; all having recourse to the art of drawing, and requiring the rules of geometry, and sometimes even those of mechanics. Moreover, it may be noticed that the labors of these different trades all contribute to one and the same end, and that it is consequently desirable that the workmen who practice them should follow a similar course of study. It will therefore often be practicable to form a special class for all employed in the building trade, including masons, stone-cutters, carpenters, smiths, joiners, and other accessory trades.

"The technical instruction to be given by drawing in this class, and which will likewise serve as applications of the rudiments of geometry and projection, will comprise the principal details of the labors of each profession. Masons and stone-cutters will learn to draw the different modes of construction to be employed, according to the nature of the materials and the parts to be executed, —simple and mixed masonry, chimneys, the different kinds of arches and their intersections, and their voussoirs and templates, staircases, &c. To these studies may also be added the actual execution, in plaster-of-Paris, of all the masonry of certain parts, on a small scale, — a proceeding which has been practised with success in certain schools of France and Germany. Carpenters and joiners will also execute working-drawings of roofs and constructions in wood; and so on with other trades.

"In towns where there are machine-workshops, it will be advantageous also to form a special class for engineers, for the purpose of making drawings of the more important portions of machines, especially of such as are peculiar to the locality, or are most used. The series of designs executed by the pupils of the schools of arts and trades may be taken as types of the mode to be adopted. The artisans engaged in the different trades working in metals may be joined to this last class, unless there should be in the neighborhood some special factories employing a great number of hands, as in the manufacture of clocks and watches, hardware, or locks; for whom a separate class ought then to be opened.

"In one word, the object of these classes being to give each workman the technical instruction required in his trade, every effort must be made to teach him to execute drawings of the articles he has to manufacture, employing them as means to make him comprehend the principles of geometry, which he will be taught at the same time. He may also be required, as an application of his knowledge, to calculate the surface, volume, and weight of the objects drawn, when their forms are not too complicated.

"It has been deemed necessary to enter somewhat minutely into these details, for the purpose of showing that this kind of instruction can only be successfully given by men who are fitted for it by their profession, or who, from enthusiasm, have devoted their attention to learning all the practical details. From this it is evident that the teachers must, for the most part, be found among engineers, architects, builders, and foremen, who, without abandoning their profession, will undertake the direction of these Sunday or evening classes. . . .

"These studies, intended for practical purposes, cannot, therefore, be efficiently directed with all the befitting details of execution, with the explanation of processes, and the necessary experiments, except by men who have themselves practised the arts whose principles and rules they have to explain, and who know how to speak the language of the ship-yard and the workshop. Hence results the impossibility of establishing for professional or industrial teaching, even from a general point of view, a uniform body of rules and methods, an organized professional staff, in short, a university of industrial education. This consequence is still more evident in all that concerns those technical studies which have for their immediate object the methods, rules, and application of the sciences.

"It is, therefore, often on the very spot where the technical instruction is to be given, or in the workshop itself, that many of the professors ought to be chosen; and, in general, they must be sought among engineers, practical men, and manufacturers."

In his report, to which reference was made in the second chapter, Prof. Leone Levi says of the canton of Geneva, Switzerland: —

"There are evening industrial schools, which, after providing for a preliminary course on arithmetic, including decimals and the metric system, have, in the inferior division, geometry, physic, and lineal design; in the middle division, algebra, book-keeping, chemistry, and industrial design; and, in the superior division, natural history, political economy, mechanics, design, descriptive geometry, and chemical manipulations. The fees in these schools are, for regular students, five francs for the preparatory course, ten francs for the inferior division, fifteen francs for the middle, and twenty francs for the superior. The fees for occasional or not regular students are five francs for the preparatory course, ten francs for the inferior division, eight francs for one course in the middle division, and ten francs for one course in the superior division. Teachers are paid in part by a fixed rate per hour, and in part by a portion of the fees, divided among all professors in proportion to the number of lessons given by each."

Prof. Leone Levi further speaks in this wise of the evening instruction which has been provided for workmen in England: —

"If, from the education of children, we pass to the instruction of those who have already entered on the active duties of life, the want now felt in this country becomes still more evident. An attempt was early made for diffusing instruction among our artisans, the foundation of mechanic institutes, the original object of which was to impart instruction to workmen in those rules and principles which lie at the basis of the art they practice; but they have failed to attract the mechanics. In the membership of mechanic institutions, the mechanics, millwrights, overlookers, spinners, and other laborers figure only in a small proportion; whilst the number taking advantage of such institutions, in proportion to the total number of laboring-classes in any one town, is quite insignificant; though it is quite possible, that, in many cases, the working-man, by contact with any such institution, becomes more enlightened and refined in manner and bearing, that, leaving his ordinary dress at home, he is in the evening little distinguishable from persons belonging to the middle class of life, and that, in many ways, the working-classes still derive from them essential benefit.

"A mechanics' institute, as usually organized, has evening classes for five evenings in the week; one evening being usually dedicated to lectures and lighter entertainments. It has a library for reference and the circulation of books, and a reading-room open from early in the morning till late at night. The subjects of instruction in the different classes are very extensive. They comprise nearly all the branches of elementary science and literature necessary for educated young men in the middle class of life, such as arithmetic, book-keeping, English composition, English grammar, English literature, drawing, and foreign languages, with some of the more advanced sciences, such as chemistry, geometry, mathematics, natural philosophy, &c.; and the fees are very low. But they are wanting in unity and system. The instruction is not consecutive: it does not extend over any definite period; whilst there is no connection whatever between the private classes and public lecturers. In fact, as schools of science and art, they are in most cases very defective; and, as to funds or modes of existence generally, their condition is most precarious, the greatest efforts being needed to maintain such institutions in existence.

"Of similar character, at least in its original object, is the Working Men's College, founded in 1854 in London. The studies there comprise drawing, vocal music, history, and law, languages ancient and modern, mathematical and physical sciences, at very low fees, and free lectures delivered on Saturday evenings by some of our most eminent men. Yet the college does not draw many of the mechanics and artisans, the greater number of students being clerks receiving very small salaries; whilst, with fees at the lowest rates, the college is not self-sustaining. The good work is in reality carried on by zealous teachers acting gratuitously; and the building itself was established by generous contributions. Nor is it to be wondered at, since even the best institutions, which appeal to the middle and higher classes, experience the greatest difficulty, and are seldom self-supporting and remunerative. The classes on those branches of study which are of acknowledged necessity, and otherwise popular, attract a sufficient number of students to allow a fair remuneration to the teachers; but those on subjects more elevated, or of more partial application, are attended by too few scholars to render it worth while either to the teacher or the institution to maintain them.

"Yet exceptions to this general rule present themselves here and there, and prominently so is the case of the evening classes at King's College, London. It is now fifteen years since, with the authority of the council of King's College, I opened (in 1852) evening courses of lectures of a practical character on commerce and commercial law. From year to year, those lectures attracted greater and increasing attention, until, in 1855, a department was established for the purpose of providing a complete system of practical instruction to young men daily employed in business, which now includes divinity, Latin, Greek, French, German and German literature, Italian, English, Spanish, Portuguese, and Hebrew language, history of England, geography, arithmetic, writing, mathematics, commerce (including principles of commerce and banking), monetary science and foreign exchanges, commercial and maritime law (national and international), drawing, elements of chemistry, practical chemistry, mechanics, physiology, botany, experimental physic, mineralogy and geology, zoölogy, political economy, public reading and speaking, law, and a civil service class. These classes have been most popular from the commencement; and from six hundred to seven hundred youths are every evening there employed in learning different branches of science, who heretofore had no opportunity to satisfy their taste, and far less to obtain the necessary erudition for the practical duties of life. King's College, situated in the very centre of this great metropolis, fulfils in this manner a most important function in the education of the adult.

"Still more recently University College, London, has established its evening classes, where Latin, Greek, Hebrew, English, French, Italian, German, geography, history, elocution, mineralogy and geology, mathematics, physic, elementary chemistry, drawing, writing, book-keeping, English law, Roman law, jurisprudence, and equity and common law, are taught by men of great ability, and at very moderate fees.

"Nor can I omit that most valuable institution, the City of London College, whose evening classes are crowded by persons belonging to the commercial houses in the city. Some of these colleges and schools may succeed in maintaining themselves, though with great difficulty; but in the majority of cases it is otherwise, and, in my opinion, there will never be a sufficient provision for the diffusion of science in this country, especially economic and commercial, natural and experimental, unless those institutions obtain a well-regulated State support."

The committee of the Hamburg (Germany) Society for the Promotion of Art and Industry say of evening schools: —

"On the fixing of a plan of lessons for a Sunday and evening school, it appears advisable, that, as far as possible, the artistic instruction should be given in the evening, and the scientific in the daytime, as it is found from experience, that, in general, workmen are too exhausted after their day's work for attention to subjects such as mathematics for instance; whilst they appear sufficiently fresh for instruction in drawing."

A committee of the Hamburg (Germany) Society for the Promotion of Art and Industry thus describe

The Museum of Industrial Products of the Royal Institution for Industry and Commerce at Stuttgart, Wurtemberg.

"This is destined to aid in the promotion of existing industries, as also to lay the foundations of industries in general; but it is in no way occupied with the promotion of any one special branch of industry.

"The principle which is the groundwork of the institution is the general aim of improving the elements of industrial occupation by exhibitions of real objects, and consequent encouragement to study, and to make these accessible to all.

"The museum contains, in spacious rooms, a rich collection of German and foreign manufactures, a great number of useful machines and implements of all kinds, an excellent collection of industrial art, a trades' drawing-school, a library, a reading-room, and a chemical laboratory.

"The collection of manufactures, arranged according to the annexed plans, contains : —

"Leather and leather work; work and carvings in wood, ivory, horn, cocoanut-shell, &c.; inlaid furniture; works in clay, cement, earthenware, and china; bricks and tiles; glass ware and glass paintings; articles made of wax, papier-maché, gutta-percha, caoutchouc, plaster, &c.; bookbinding and portfolio-makers' wares; brushes; paint-brushes; combs; basket-work in straw, osier, and reeds; patterns of clothing and ready-made clothes; nets and hooks; fabrics, and fabrics in process, made of wool, silk, cotton, flax, hemp, jute, &c.; colors; chemicals; combustibles; pencils; oils; glue; instruments for measuring, measures, scales and weights; implements for drawing; apparatus used in cooking, in the house, for lighting, warming, and extinguishing; agricultural and garden tools; locks and keys; door and window fastenings; works in tin and copper, &c.

"On account of their origin, we must particularly notice the many patterns of printed, embroidered, and woven stuffs, as well as of paper-hangings. There are business-houses in Paris who receive subscriptions for the supply of all the new patterns brought out, and who furnish annually to their subscribers from two hundred to four hundred specimens. The Royal Wurtemberg Industrial and Art Department is in correspondence with such a house, Messrs. T. C. Claude Brothers, 32 Rue du Sentier, Paris, and pays, for example, two hundred and fifty francs annually for about three hundred new patterns of hangings. The patterns are tolerably large; and from them drawings might be made for other purposes. All the patterns are bound together, with a notice of the price and plan of origin, and form a valuable portion of the library, which is more especially useful to merchants. T. C. Claude Brothers undertake, among other things, subscriptions for drawings of the most modern Parisian furniture.

"Apart from this collection of manufactures, the division for machines and implements is to be found in an opposite room.

"As motive-powers to set in motion the other machines, there are exhibited, a caloric machine, a machine moved by gas (by Lenoir), a two-horse locomotive, as well as a stationary steam-engine. After them are placed in rows articles of machinery; viz., a collection of English castings, such as water and steam cocks, pumps, level indicators, balances, valves, grease boxes, gas apparatus, dyanometers, &c. Farther on are articles of wrought and cast iron, hydraulic and other presses, an hydraulic crane (Heberviude), a screw windlass, machine for raising water, fire-engines, weights, flour and crushing mills, looms, boring-machines, implements for drilling and turning, machines for hammering and planing, implements for various trades, &c. Besides these, there are machines and contrivances for helping in household works, sewing-machines, washing and drying machines, apparatus for filling and corking bottles, beer-pumps, &c.

"The industrial art division of the exhibition numbers nearly a thousand beautiful works, executed, for the most part, by the newest processes of art printing. These are arranged according to trades, and contain works of ornamentation and art industry, for mechanicians, builders, joiners, paper-hangers, coach-builders, house-painters, workers in metal, earthenware manufacturers, as well as embroidery and other needleworkers, for weaving, book-printing, and instruction in drawing.

"There are also exhibited a quantity of photographic pictures, and a great collection of price-catalogues and price-lists, which, besides giving information as to prices, and plans of origin, help also in the drawing-up of similar catalogues.

"A great part of this collection is made up by the apparatus for instruction; and here we may particularly mention with approbation the rich collection of plaster and paper copies, as well as the plaster figures for the drawing-school. This collection, from the way in which it is arranged, gives also an opportunity of studying the various styles of art.

"The public drawing-school is annexed to the industrial art collection, and has already been mentioned in the first part of this report. This is attended by artisans, who use the collections for their own special callings, and also by those learning art industries, but especially by the teachers who wish to perfect themselves for giving instruction in drawing. We may particularly mention, that, in the industrial art division, artisans receive artistic instruction gratis, and make diligent use of it.

"The chemical laboratory which is annexed to the exhibition has the aim of making experiments as to new discoveries in the department of chemical industry, as well as of undertaking the execution of analyses. Of these, from five hundred to six hundred are made annually for manufacturers, and at very moderate prices, — almost under cost price.

"The not inconsiderable library of the exhibition, which embraces the department of industrial activity and commerce, is much used, as also the reading-room, in which about seventy periodicals relating to industrial, commercial, and economical subjects, are taken in, as also the directories of large commercial towns, and a list of the patents granted in England and America. Lastly, there is in the neighborhood of the exhibition a weaving school, with looms, which need merely be mentioned here.

"One department of the exhibition, which in its foundation was incorporated with it, has for some time ceased to exist: this is the department for the exhibition of the industrial products of Wurtemberg.

"This was intended to make foreign merchants acquainted with the home manufactures, and to promote their sale. Native manufacturers were not allowed admittance, in order, as far as possible, to protect the exhibiter from the imitation of new fabrics by competitors.

"Against all expectation, this department did not attain the desired aim.

"The Royal Department for Industry and Commerce possesses a yearly revenue of ninety thousand florins, of which thirty thousand florins are annually expended in acquisitions for the exhibition.

"This is open, on working-days and holidays, from ten to twelve o'clock in the morning, and from two to six o'clock in the afternoon. All persons who visit it for the purposes of their trade, and who will enter their names in a book placed for that purpose, have free admittance. Others pay six kreutz entrance. On Sundays, from half-past ten till half-past twelve o'clock, admittance is free, without exception.

"The loan of patterns and of articles in the industrial art collection was particularly mentioned at Stuttgart, and pointed out as being especially advantageous.

"That the influence of the exhibition is most salutary, as also that it has effected a decided progress in the industry of Wurtemberg, all the manufacturers of the country would no doubt unanimously admit. How extensively it is made use of, is to be seen from the fact that a third part of the collections is lent out at one time, and serves for the thorough instruction of the workmen. Let us reflect how long it often is before a small manufacturer (and it is exactly this numerous class of persons which needs support) can be made acquainted with new technical improvements, and can get to see them; how long he continues to work with forms of which the fashion has already become antiquated, and uses instruments which have long been replaced by more convenient ones; let us think how important any movement is to the manufacturer which furnishes him with new ideas, and how necessary it is in the present day, for the success of even the most skilled workman, that he should introduce novelties into the market, — we can then imagine how grateful the hundreds of workpeople are to the Wurtemberg Museum, which is of such service to them in their instruction, and the promotion of their trades."

In chapter two mention is made of the reports of the English artisans who were sent gratuitously to the Paris Exhibition, 1867. One of these artisans, Mr. Charles Alfred Hooper, cabinet-maker, says of museums: —

"The boys serve three or four years in the trade, and have better advantages for getting an art education than we have. All the schools are open to them, where the higher branches are taught; and they are not kept, as our boys, to simply reading, writing, and arithmetic. The art galleries and museums are all open free to them Sundays and week days, so that they imbibe a taste for art and refined behavior before they can read or write."

Another, Mr. Aaron Green, porcelain decorator, says: —

"The show-rooms and museum at Sèvres are, perhaps, the greatest treat which a porcelain painter could be favored with: there he can see specimens of every country and style. And they are not mere specimens; but many of them are of the rarest quality and value. The porcelain painting exhibited in the show-rooms here is not equalled by any in the Great Exhibition, and is of such surpassing excellence as to warrant the French in assuming a superiority over any other nation. The painting of some of the figure subjects is truly grand; while the fruit and flower painting of Jaccober it seems impossible to surpass: indeed, I have never seen any thing that at all approaches it. There are large vases covered with ornament, which for beauty, distribution, and purity of form and color, filled me with amazement, and a feeling somewhat approaching to humiliation.

"I think there can be no doubt but that the close proximity of the workshops to the museum must be of immense value to the decorators and designers, refreshing their memory, inciting their ideas, and continually adding to their stock of knowledge. And in this instance the French teach us a lesson; for, while the examples purchased from time to time by the nation are very valuable and instructive, they would be of more use and real service, if, instead of being assembled in the metropolis, each locality that is pre-eminently famous for some speciality had its own museum. I think by this means our national industry would be benefited, and the general prosperity of the nation increased; for it is obvious, that, under the present system, our artisans (at best) can see the examples they need only at rare intervals; and that often, when they wish to make use of them, they have to depend upon recollections considerably weakened by time, and consequently of a very imperfect character."

Another, Mr. Benjamin Lucraft, chair-maker, says: —

"I will now, in as few words as possible, offer two or three suggestions whereby this state of things may be altered, and the art workmen of England enabled so to improve themselves in matters of taste as to successfully compete with the now more fortunate workmen of France. In the first place, the council of the Society of Arts may use its influence with her Majesty's Government for the establishment of local museums of art manufacture, with lecture-halls, libraries, and other necessary adjuncts and appliances, for the use and instruction of the people, and open at such hours as will suit their convenience and opportunities for attending; which, as a matter of course, will be in the evening, when lectures by competent men would be largely attended; and I venture to suggest that the leading industries of certain districts may form their principal feature. In this way, if for the north of London a museum should be established, its position ought to be as near as possible the centre of its manufacturing district; and the most important industries of that district should be especially considered in the fitting-up, and the specimens to be exhibited. For example, to assist the cabinet-makers, carvers, chair-makers, and upholsterers of Shoreditch, Hoxton, and Lower Islington, — where this trade is carried on to a great extent, — good specimens of different styles and times in these branches would be of the greatest value; and in the adjoining parishes of St. Luke and Clerkewell, where tens of thousands of the population are dependent on the trade of the watchmaker, the jeweller, the gold and silver workers, and all the various trades connected with the precious metals, examples of these, from the earliest times, and from all countries, would be of the greatest interest and benefit, not only to them, but to the whole nation."

Another, Mr. James Mackie, wood-carver, says: —

"The education of the workman is of primary importance. Our schools have rendered valuable service; and much of our progress is traceable to their influence; but they are capable of doing more, if only a new life is infused into them. Our great buildings are full of excellent examples, which deserve to be more studied than they are. In our museums and galleries there are splendid examples of art, that, if studied, would work wonderful changes in our taste and power. I know that they are not esteemed as they should be; and I also know that they are not so accessible as they should be. Establish more museums of industrial art, be they ever so small, and let them be open at convenient hours and days for the artisan class. Let the architects look to the carving that is being done in our new London; for much of it is a scandal and a disgrace to our taste, and its effects upon the carver's education are most damaging. Something better is demanded. If we are to have any art in our streets, pray let it be good and instructive. Let us have open spaces in the metropolis arranged to please the eye and develop the taste; and at the same time provide the means of rest for those who do not want the accommodation supplied in places of resort that are questionable. Do not forget that the education of the workman is

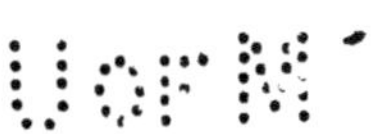

not confined to the established schools; for there are many ways of increasing his knowledge outside the walls of those useful places. Let the workman be encouraged to learn and practise the arts of drawing, modelling, and design; for they undoubtedly constitute the very groundwork of the carver's art. Let the encouragement be kind, friendly, and continuous, taking the form of liberal prizes to the advanced workmen, accompanied with numerous small prizes, in order to develop the industry of all. Lectures on art would be of great value; for men would be by them induced to study, and put forth their strength. Let our system of instruction and practice at our schools be simple, inviting, and interesting, not dull, repulsive, and crushing, as it certainly has been to many. We have the stuff amongst us: let it be cared for in a large and liberal spirit, and it will be strange indeed if the England of the future does not see something more worthy of her great name."

Another, Mr. Thomas Jacob, cabinet draughtsman, says:—

"To improve the taste of working-men, every possible opportunity should be given them of inspecting works of art during their leisure hours, that they may see what has been and is being done by the artists, who are but men like themselves. It is unreasonable to expect a man to imitate or rival that which he has never seen; but after he has seen these things, if he has talent and mettle of the right sort in him, he will not long be content to lag behind his fellow workmen of this or any other country."

Mr. J. Scott Russell, in his book, "Systematic Technical Education of the English people," says:—

"The two words 'look there,' are often more valuable than an hour's lecture. The pupil takes into his mind the form, color, meaning, of the thing itself, which no words could give him: and, in good collections of this sort, the insides of things are shown him as clearly as the outsides; so that the pupil's knowledge is thorough, instead of merely skin-deep. It should also be remembered that education by the eye is as fertile in fruit as education by the ear; and that merely to familiarize men with the sight of things made as they should be is the most effectual teaching to avoid and dislike what is inferior or wrong. The material element of teaching is, therefore, secondary only in value to the living element."

UNIVERSAL PRIMARY EDUCATION.

The French Imperial Commission described in the second chapter elicited the following from the editors of "The Journal of Professional Education," as to the elementary education of artisans: —

"There is no doubt that one of the first indispensable requirements in children who are to receive a professional training is a knowledge of the elements of the science, — such as geometry, physics, and chemistry, — in a degree adapted to the wants of any special industry. For this purpose, schools on the plan of the Turgot School should be multiplied in the great manufacturing centres, Paris, Lyons, Nantes, Bordeaux, Lille, and Mulhouse. A preliminary training of this description is required even by children who are destined for the handicrafts. Every manufacturer knows the difference between an apprentice who has been thoroughly accustomed to scientific definitions, and one who can merely read and write: even in learning the use of tools, the former is twice as quick as the latter besides understanding more easily the explanation of the master."

In their report the French Imperial Commission say:—

"In fact, the failure of the first foundations of this kind attempted in England, about 1825, under the name of 'Mechanics Institutes,' like those which since 1800 have succeeded in Scotland under the direction of Dr. Birkbeck, who was their first founder, proves that it is of paramount importance, first of all, to make sure that the workmen for whom the lectures are intended have received as sound and complete a primary education as possible. Thus whilst, in Scotland, the Parochial Schools had spread among all classes of the population an amount of instruction about equal to that which the French law of 1833 defined as *superior primary instruction*, the day and evening classes of the Mechanics' Institutes obtained a complete and almost general success. In England, on the contrary, the teachers in these institutions had scarcely begun to talk of science to the mechanics, when they encountered an obstacle which had not been found to exist in Scotland to the same extent. The absence of elementary instruction was complete. Lord Brougham and his friends were in advance of their age. . . . Of these institutions there soon remained nothing but the name and the building; which last was used for other purposes. In most cases, it was occupied by a mechanics' or middle-class club, where persons who paid a small monthly contribution met to amuse themselves on winter evenings. There was no such thing as teaching."

In their summary of the inquiry on technical education in Germany and Switzerland, the sub-commission of the French Imperial Commission speak thus:—

"In the first place, and almost with one accord, all the persons consulted have recognized and insisted on the necessity of a degree of general preparatory instruction proportioned to the extent of professional or industrial education which is to be its complement; and which is intended to place every individual in a position to follow with success the career he may have in view, or has already embraced. But at the same time it has been as positively declared by the most eminent principals of industrial establishments, that the deplorable and far too general absence of primary instruction among even the most intelligent workmen was one of the greatest and most lamentable obstacles to the development of their faculties, and the progress of industry. . . .

"The course to be followed, and the different means to be employed, to improve and extend the education of workingmen already engaged in the practice of their trades, have been among the most important objects of the inquiry. The difficulties thrown in the way of this kind of instruction by the almost total absence of primary education, and especially by the general ignorance of the scientific forms of even the simplest reasoning, have been pointed out to the commission However, numerous examples tend to show, that, by combining the study of drawing with the teaching peculiar to the different industries, it is not impossible to obtain happy results. The man who is in the habit of working any given substance, often, indeed, acquires by a sort of intuition a sounder and more intimate knowledge of its fundamental properties and mechanical effects than he who has limited his studies to the desk."

In chapter two, reference is made to the report of Prof. Leone Levi. He says: —

"Hitherto, the progress of Britain in industry and manufacture has been achieved by a few leading minds operating with an army of laborers wonderfully endowed with physical and moral power to overcome the greatest resistance, yet singularly deficient in intellectual power. Incomparably greater would be her progress, were science and art more diffused amongst the entire community. What is required, therefore, is, first, a more extended and comprehensive system of primary and secondary instruction, well arranged, and adapted to the requirements of society; and, secondly, the diffusion of technical instruction, or instruction in those sciences and arts which enter into the different occupations and professions of life, altogether direct and practical in its teaching, and everywhere associated with the realities of life."

Mr. James Hole, honorable secretary of the Yorkshire Union of Mechanics' Institutes, in a letter to Lord Robert Montagu, vice-president of the Committee of Council on Education, England, says: —

"All who have expressed any opinions on this question concur in thinking that we must have a much more complete system of primary instruction before secondary education can become developed and improved to a satisfactory degree. For many years past, the greater part of the educational work of our mechanics' institutions has been to supply the mere elementary education that ought to have been acquired in the day school; and the great object for which mechanics' institutions were originally established — viz., the technical education now so much talked about — has remained almost in total abeyance."

"In his reply to Lord Stanley, Mr. Lumley encloses

a report on popular education in Switzerland, which thus speaks of primary education: —

"Instruction in the Swiss primary schools comprises reading and writing in the mother-tongue (German, French, or Italian, according to the canton), arithmetic, and the first principles of geometry, drawing, singing, Swiss and general history, geography, and the elements of natural science. Gymnastics are also being gradually introduced; and female needlework is taught to the girls at fixed hours in the girls' and mixed schools."

Mr. J. Scott Russell, in his work on "The Systematic Technical Education of the English People," says: —

"Unhappily, mechanics, when taught to working-men, is generally either taught superficially, unphilosophically, or with little or no reference to the business of their life. Economy of bodily strength, best ways of handling things, best ways of moving things, best ways of helping each other, best ways of carrying, lifting, shifting things, — these are seldom taught. Some foolish algebraical formula, or abstract geometrical diagram, is put before the poor mechanic, and called science. As well call it magic. . . .

"I am hopeless in the matter of educating the 'working-man' who has grown up into manhood without education. For the most part, such men are too old to learn. I have never seen, but exceptionally, much good come of trying to drive figures and geometrical problems, and mechanical theorems, and light and shade, into the head of a full-grown workman who had failed to get a good education when young. There have been brilliant exceptions — how brilliant! how few!"

CHAPTER VI.

DRAWING.

THE evidence which is presented in this chapter, coming from many and the most trustworthy sources, shows beyond reasonable doubt, that among all the branches of instruction, from the lowest to the highest, which can contribute to the technical education of either sex, drawing, in its varied forms and applications, is the one most essential to make common. As, in teaching other things, somewhat different methods are successfully followed, so the evidence shows, as was to be expected, that somewhat different methods are successfully followed in teaching drawing. While there are methods which receive the universal condemnation of good educators, there are other methods which receive their universal approval, though not in the same degree. The methods must, of course, vary, more or less, according to the age of the pupils, according to the circumstances under which the instruction is given, and according to the particular result which it is desired to attain. The following points appear to be clearly settled: —

1. There is such an intimate relation between the different departments of drawing and art, while broad culture is always so much better than narrow culture, that the best results in any one direction can be secured only when the instruction is general. To become a thorough master of any department of drawing or art, one needs to be acquainted with all departments. Hence the instruction in drawing should be, whenever possible, broad, and not simply special, even when special results alone are sought.

2. As it is impossible that every one should be thoroughly instructed in all the departments of drawing, it is well, in determining what the public schools should attempt, to divide drawing into three general courses: a preparatory course, an industrial course, and an artistic course. The preparatory course, embracing the elements of both industrial and artistic drawing, should be pursued by all pupils alike. When this course — whch should be quite liberal, extending at least through the grammar school — has been finished, those pupils of the high school who are to engage in industrial pursuits, but have not time to take both the industrial and artistic courses, should give special, though not exclusive, atten-

tion to projection and working drawings. For a similar reason, those pupils of the high school who desire to obtain a more purely artistic culture will give special attention to shading and perspective, to drawing the human figure, and from nature. As it is not the proper business of the public schools to make specialists, the instruction in the industrial course should be, in the main, confined to those things which the different industries have in common. So, too, the instruction in the artistic course should be, in the main, confined to those things only which belong alike to the different artistic professions. Those things which specially belong to any one industry, or to any one department of art, and are therefore of limited use, should usually be left to special schools.

3. In its general character the instruction should be rational, not dogmatic; that is, the pupils should be taught the reason for what they do, so that every drawing, every line they make, will be an expression of intelligence. With rare exceptions, the teacher need not, and the judicious teacher will not, give young pupils things to do which involve principles clearly beyond the range of their comprehension. When this must be done, then the less said about the principles the better: of necessity the instruction must, in such case, degenerate into dogmatism. Dogmatic instruction

will simply enable the pupils to do again what they have once done, — a thing of great value indeed; but rational instruction, giving a mastery of principles, will not only enable the pupils to do again what they have once done, but to make new applications of the principles learned. It should be the aim to produce workmen, designers, artists, who can do something more than imitate; who, working in obedience to fundamental principles, can meet the ever-changing requirements of actual life, can give the world original creations. Those pupils whose instruction in drawing simply enables them to copy have been poorly instructed indeed; and the instruction will tell adversely upon their future careers.

4. There are two general and very different modes which are followed in the execution of drawings. The first lays great stress upon fine finish, less upon expression; the lines are drawn with the utmost care from the outset; and the shading is elaborately executed with a pencil-point. The last lays great stress upon expression, less upon fine finish; the lines are drawn boldly from the outset, it being left to time and practice to give accuracy; while the shading is rapidly done with the stump. The first, which may be called the English method, tends to produce workmen, designers, and artists who work slowly, and finish finely, but whose

work is lacking in life and character. The second, which may be called the French method, gives rapid execution, and yields products, which, while oftentimes lacking in finish, are always instinct with life and character. The preference is given to the latter method both for purely artistic and for industrial purposes. But evidently the best method must aim to secure both finish and expression with celerity of execution. Any product which is both well designed and well finished must command a better price than if it is only well designed or only well finished.

5. From time to time, teachers should vary somewhat their method of instruction. They should accustom their pupils to use different materials; as the blackboard, which permits such freedom of movement, should occasionally take the place of paper. They should not always require their pupils to draw from the flat, nor always from objects, nor always from the human figure. Indeed, the instruction should be judiciously graduated, with ever something of variety for the purpose both of better pleasing and better disciplining.

6. After a little preliminary practice in the drawing and division of lines, pupils should begin with exercises in drawing from flat copies, which should be symmetrically regular; that is, geometrical or conventionalized forms, without perspective and without shading. These exer-

cises should be continued long enough to familiarize the learner with pure form; to familiarize him with the leading principles of design, especially as applied to textile fabrics and to all flat ornamentation; to familiarize him with the different styles of decorative art, both ancient and modern. The copies, therefore, should be largely historical, and the most beautiful it is possible to select. When the pupils have thus become acquainted with what has been done, and have learned the principles according to which it was done, they will be prepared not only to reproduce intelligently, but to originate intelligently: indeed, while they are working at their copies, they should be constantly required to produce new designs, which they will be both able and pleased to do, and thus will become much more than mere copyists. Again: the taste of the pupils — especially if "taste is the recollection of the beautiful," as it has been defined — must be greatly improved by the long study of such beautiful forms as the copies will furnish.

When the pupils have learned to draw regular forms, which permit them to verify their work and to determine whether their drawings are accurate or not, then, and not till then, should they begin to draw irregular forms, like those in nature, which do not permit them to verify their work and determine whether or not their drawings are accurate. If the pupils cannot learn to draw regular forms accurately, it is absurd to expect that they will ever learn to draw accurately forms which are irregular. Until they are able to do the first with a good degree of success, they should not be set about doing the second. The symmetrical should therefore precede the unsymmetrical: that which can be verified should precede that which cannot be verified. A little intermixture, perhaps, of the latter with the former, for the sake of variety, may not be objectionable. But when it comes to drawing from nature, from unsymmetrical objects, what should be the general character of such drawing in the public schools? As a chief reason for putting drawing into the public schools must be industrial, it is evident that those natural objects should be first taken which have the most to do with practical art. It is the vegetable world, not the animal world, nor the human figure, from which practical art, both ancient and modern, has derived the greater portion of its principles and its designs. It is particularly appropriate, therefore, that pupils in the public schools should first learn to draw those vegetable forms — leaves, flowers, vines — which have contributed so much to practical art. Useful as it undoubtedly is, especially in the matter of discipline, to draw the human figure, yet it is an indirect and laborious way of reaching practical results. Indeed, it may well be questioned whether satisfactory results can ever be reached in this way alone, as some have claimed.

7. Taken at the proper time, but not at the outset, it is clear that drawing from geometrical models and beautiful artificial objects, from beautiful ornaments in relief, and from graceful casts, is of the most unquestionable value, both industrial and purely artistic. The pupils thus learn to represent on paper objects having the three dimensions. For industrial purposes, the value consists mainly in disciplining the imagination, training the eye, and improving the taste. Every artisan should be so thoroughly trained in this species of drawing as to be able to see mentally the exact form of any object he is required to construct, determining at once the direction of each line. If it is a beautiful object that is required, he should be able to make it, which he can never do unless he is first able to discriminate between what is, and what is not, beautiful. This species of drawing involves somewhat of perspective, of light and shade, — things which are indirectly of much industrial value, while they lead directly to the highest artistic results.

8. Drawing with instruments, which is almost wholly practical in its applications, can and should be taught in the public schools. While the great object is to train

the hand and eye, to teach the principles of design, to discipline the judgment and cultivate the taste, by freehand drawing, yet the industrial applications of drawing, which can only be mastered by the use of instruments, are so many, and so exceedingly important, that the ruler, triangle, compasses, and bow-pen, if nothing more, should find a place in all public schools except the primary. The evidence shows that children from ten to thirteen years of age, if properly taught, can be made to comprehend, and to execute with instruments, not only linear drawings, based on plane geometry, but working-drawings, which involve the principles of projection, and are based on descriptive geometry. It is very essential that each artisan should know enough of the principles of projection to be able at least to read the working-drawings which are placed in his hand, if he has not skill enough to make such drawings. Very few American artisans, whether carpenters, ship-builders, masons, machinists, or others, now know enough to do this; and so they are obliged to work under constant supervision, and at reduced wages. It is not the business of the common schools to make draughtsmen, but to teach all enough of the theory and applications of projection to meet this universal want of artisans. The finished draughtsmen must be the product of the special schools. A knowledge of perspective, which is the drawing of objects as they appear, is most readily obtained after a knowledge of projection (orthographic), which is the drawing of objects as they are. Even the artist, therefore, is served by a knowledge of the general principles involved in working-drawings. Again: there is no one of either sex who can well afford to dispense with the peculiar discipline which is derived from instrumental drawing. The use of instruments should alternate with freehand practice.

9. The pupils should not be wholly dependent on the teacher for instruction, as some have thought it best they should be. Above the primary schools a printed text should go with all the copies (whether the copies are in books or on charts), and with all models (whether for freehand or instrumental practice). This text, carefully prepared, will afford a clearer explanation than can usually be given off-hand by the teacher; and, further, the pupils can go over it again and again until it is fully comprehended. With a text for their guidance, the pupils can make much more rapid and more intelligent progress than they can possibly make without it; while the labor of the teacher is thereby greatly diminished. Even with a good text in the hands of his pupils, the teacher will find enough to do in the teaching of drawing, as he finds enough to do in teaching arithmetic, his

pupils having a book for their guidance. The teacher must often give dictation-exercises, that the pupils may learn to imagine the form of a drawing from the oral description, as, in actual life, they must frequently imagine the forms of objects from oral descriptions. The pupils having executed the drawings, each according to his interpretation of the oral description, the teacher then places the drawing on the blackboard, that the pupils may see whether they interpreted the oral description correctly. Again: the teacher should often exercise the pupils in reproducing from memory drawings previously executed, whether from flat copies or from models. But, after making due allowance for all methods and devices, the progress of the pupils will be greatly accelerated if each has a text telling how to execute the given exercises, and describing the principles of drawing and designing. Indeed, it should never be forgotten that one of the great objects of early education is to teach pupils to use books readily, in order that they may continue to advance in their studies after leaving school, when they have no teacher to direct, but must rely wholly upon books. To-day very few American artisans are able to obtain instruction from even the best prepared book, because they find it so difficult to interpret printed language.

10. Like the flat copies, the models and other objects

placed before the pupils should be the most beautiful it is possible to obtain. Well-appointed museums which can be frequently visited by the pupils will greatly aid in the development of correct taste. So, too, the taste will be decidedly influenced by the architecture which comes under the daily observation.

11. When logical demonstration can be supplemented, as often it may be, by graphic demonstration, the understanding of any subject is always rendered much easier. For this reason, the power to draw is of great service to the teacher, and should be acquired by every one who aims to do the best work in the schoolroom. When acquired, it should be frequently used for the amusement and instruction of the pupils in various branches of study.

THE FRENCH IMPERIAL COMMISSION.

[See Chap 2, for particulars about the French Imperial Commission, to whom what follows for a number of pages is accredited.]

In his evidence before the commission, Rev. Father Baudine, assistant superior of the Christian Brothers' School, says: —

"A series of drawing copy-books was published in 1860, adapted to popularize the drawing of ornament in all schools, from the village school to the middle-class school of large towns. In the method adopted in giving this elementary instruction in the drawing of ornament, care is taken to select copies on good grounds only; that is to say, either on the score of taste or style. Every study, every fragment, has a name attached to it, giving the character of the style to which it belongs. Thus, after going through the course of copy-books, the pupil can easily distinguish between Grecian, Roman, Byzantine, Gothic, Renaissance, &c., orders of ornamentation, and is even sufficiently advanced to make an original design belonging to one of those orders.

"Drawing from the cast, and modelling, naturally follows on that of ornament; but the little time which the junior pupils can devote to the subject permits this branch to be carried on only in the adult evening classes. To ornamental drawing ought to be added geometrical drawing; being of much more importance to the working-classes. The method adopted in teaching this subject consists in hanging up before the class a large sheet, four feet by three, containing copies of joiner's work, upholstery, carpentry, architecture, and machines. The pupils have by them figured sketches of these copies so as to be able to reproduce on their books these copies to any required scale. By this means, a class of from fifty to sixty, and even a hundred, pupils can work at the same subject, and follow the explanations of the teacher. To facilitate still more the study of this subject, and in order that the pupils may have a better knowledge of what objects they reproduce, they have set before them solid models of the same objects as are on the large sheets, — some in wood, others in plaster or cast metal. The models are cut by vertical or horizontal planes; so that the details for the drawing are better understood. To these models others are added to be handled by the pupils themselves, that they may make sketches of them, with different elevations and plans. By this means it has been found possible to make children of from ten to thirteen years understand the theory of projections."

In his evidence before the commission, M. Delahaye, director of the Professional School at Batignolles, member of the Council of Head Masters of the Department of the Seine, thus expresses himself: —

"Great importance is attached to the teaching of drawing, so much so, that the boys of seven years old commence to learn drawing at the same time that they begin to learn to write. A peculiar method is adopted in this subject, which might, with advantage, be adopted in the primary schools. Paper ruled in squares is used; so that, by the aid merely of the ruler and pen, a child can make many different drawings; which, it must be confessed, are not very artistic, but which accustom him to neatness, give him a notion of symmetry, and educate his taste. When these children come afterwards to the use of the compass and bow-pen, and to tint their drawings, their hand is practised, and often very skilful."

In his evidence before the commission, M. Bardin, professor of Industrial Drawing to the Communal Schools of the City of Paris, says: —

"All the models that are put before them are accompanied by a descriptive text. Each of them comprehends and retains what he studies. He can work alone. The professor has only to correct the work, or to explain a point which has not been understood at first. These models, thus explained, have an immense advantage over an engraving which does not even bear an indication of the drawing that it represents; besides which, a text accompanying a drawing is always more precise than the oral description that the master can give to each pupil, and helps to keep alive the remembrance of it."

In his evidence before the commission, M. Lequien, director of the Communal School of Drawing in the Rue Ménilmontant, Paris, says: —

"I believe instruction in these subjects (linear and architectural drawing) to be indispensable to all engaged in the manufacture of furniture. Cabinet-making particularly would derive great benefit, both as regards the proportions, elegance, and purity of form, as well as regards the harmony of the mouldings, which are often disproportionate, or of different styles. A piece of furniture, no matter what it may be, — whether a cabinet, sideboard, bed, or console, — is nothing but an edifice applied to a useful purpose. Architectural design should rule the whole as well as the details; and it is from the judicious combinations of these elements, arranged with a view to its use, that it derives its merit. Furniture destined for repose ought to be of simple construction: the ornaments with which it is often overloaded appear to be made rather to hide the clumsiness of its form than to embellish it. Ought not the furniture of a room to agree both in shape and color with the architecture? It is a whole, each part of which should be in harmony. In this last part of the work the architect is often replaced by the paper-hanger, who, having no architectural or decorative knowledge, allows himself to be guided by the extravagant caprices of fashion or by a traditional routine. Again: bronzes, lustres, candelabras, cups, and the basement of a clock, may all be considered in relation to their architectural fitness. Ceramic art borrows its first and principal value from form. No matter how great the merit of the paintings which ornament porcelain, it is the proportion and the elegance of the shape which ought to be the first consideration. In monumental art, statuary itself is subordinate, in its proportions and its effect, to the laws of the science of lines, which ought to prevail in every manufacture."

In his evidence before the commission, M. Gerardon, founder and director of the Central School at Lyons, professor at La Martinière School, says: —

"The method by which descriptive geometry is taught is also peculiar, and well worthy of notice. For this study each pupil is furnished with a small tin box about eight inches long, four inches broad, and three-quarters of an inch in depth. This box is filled with yellow wax, prepared so as not to turn hard. It represents to the pupil the horizontal plane of projection. The edge opposite to him is the ground line; and he can imagine for himself the plane of elevation passing through this ground line. Small strips of iron wire serve to represent lines in space, the projections on the horizontal plane by laying them on the box, and those on the plane of elevation by fixing them on the edge which represents the ground line. The movement of these strips is effected by direction of the teacher; and the pupil is enabled easily to understand a diagram in descriptive geometry.

"Instruction in drawing consists of machine-drawing in perspective and projection, as well as of the method of tinting. At first the pupil draws on his slate to facilitate correction, and avoid waste of paper. The first models which he has to draw from are figures in iron wire, representing cubes, prisms, pyramids, &c.: then he draws parts of machines, and finally complete machines. Afterwards he proceeds to drawing projections, first in figured sketches, and then in drawings to scale: finally he completes his studies by learning to tint. The pupils are arranged in a circle round the model, which is placed on a stand in the midst of them. They are seated on stools carrying a stage to support the slate or drawing-board. There is also a class for modelling and moulding; but it is not numerously attended. . . .

"At the Central School, as at La Martinière, the pupil, from his first entrance, begins to draw in perspective from models: then he passes quickly to projection, which is more closely connected with the labor of the workshop. As soon as he has acquired sufficient skill, the following plan is pursued: A model is placed before twelve or fourteen pupils; the teacher takes it to pieces before them, explains the principal arrangements, draws attention to the different forms, and, after having given all necessary explanations, removes the model. The pupil must then execute from memory, and without instruments, sketches of the whole, and of the details and sections required by the teacher. When the time fixed for the execution of this drawing from memory has elapsed, the model is replaced before the pupils: the teacher points out the corrections to be made; and a pupil placed close to the model takes all the measurements, and dictates the dimensions. The model is once more removed; and from the sketch the pupil must now make a drawing to scale. This kind of work, and a little drawing of ornament, and practice in tinting, constitute the study of the first year. During the second and third year, the pupils, while continuing from time to time the drawing from memory, pass on to another kind of study. Drawings of machines are given to them, but not to be servilely copied: they are required to draw a section on a line marked on the drawing. In this way the pupil can never copy a drawing without understanding it: he must analyze it in all its particulars for himself. To others, again, is given a drawing, — as, for example, of a steam-engine, — taken from some work on machinery, together with the text which accompanies it. The teacher explains to the pupil a certain portion of the machine, — the cylinder, for instance, — with the arrangement of its parts: the latter must then draw every piece of it (as if it were taken completely to pieces) to a certain fixed scale. When this work is finished, the copy is removed; and the pupil must proceed to draw the whole from the drawings which he has already made of the parts. In these two divisions the young men are also practised in making designs of parts of machines according to the principles of the strength of materials, which they have learned in school; designs for boilers according to the principles of physics; designs of machines or of buildings of all kinds, as applications of the sciences which they have studied at school. As a supplement to the study of drawing, the pupils of the second and third years visit, every Thursday, certain manufactories which are fixed upon, and must bring back figured sketches of some of the machines: these they must afterwards reproduce as finished drawings to scale. Afterwards, from all these drawings, a selection is made of those which possess most interest, or are of the greatest utility; and, these being lithographed, an album is made, intended specially for the use of the pupils of the school."

In his evidence before the commission, M. Malet, professor at the Imperial Artillery School at Douai, says: —

"The class in drawing meets every day from half-past twelve to two o'clock. Formerly it used to meet from five to seven; and probably the old arrangement will be resumed, as it had the advantage of accustoming the pupils to draw both by artificial light and by daylight. The class contains about seventy or eighty pupils, of from thirteen to fourteen years of age. As to the method of instruction, it is that which is generally adopted: the basis is the study of the figure, and effect is obtained by line shading. But this method, though good in principle, is, in the opinion of M. Malet, not one which is to be recommended for those who are not fine-art students, but have need of the power of sketching rapidly and accurately. He would wish to see introduced three divisions — one preparatory, another industrial, and the third artistic — for the students who wish to become artists, and aspire to the Fine Art School (*École des Beaux Arts*)."

In his evidence before the commission M. Gouin, civil engineer, Paris, says: —

"Nothing is more difficult to form than a machine designer and mechanical engineer. A hundred engineers for making railways can be found before one who can make a good machine is discovered. To become a good mechanical engineer great patience is required: five or six years must be passed in a drawing office, and a year or two in making tracings, so as to know a machine as a whole, as well as its details, and not to be obliged to have recourse to calculation or drawings to know how to trace a piece which has to be made. Just as an artist is not compelled to measure every time the proportion of the head to the body to make a correct study of the figure, but has it all in his eye, so a machine designer ought to have in his head all the relations of the different parts of a machine. This knowledge is only acquired after a prolonged examination of excellent models."

In their elaborate report, based upon their wide investigations, the Imperial Commission say: —

"One immediate conclusion from the facts above stated is, that drawing, in all its applications, may and must be regarded as one of the simplest and most direct means which technical education can employ; since it renders visible to the eye, and perceptible to the mind, most of the propositions of elementary and descriptive geometry with their applications, and likewise affords the means of submitting to calculation many mechanical phenomena and the proportions of the constituent parts of machines. Moreover, in all that concerns the art of construction, drawing familiarizes the pupil with execution and with the proportions which science or practice have sanctioned.

"All these considerations have led the commission to propose: —

"1. That, for the instruction of apprentices and workmen, it is advisable to encourage, in preference to purely oral lectures, the establishment of regular classes to be held especially on Sundays or in the evenings of working-days.

"2. That this teaching should not be at all dogmatical, but should make it a rule to explain in the simplest possible manner the principles of science by the aid of facts, and by showing their application.

"3. Lastly, that drawing, with all its applications to the different industrial arts, should be considered as the *principal* means to be employed in technical instruction. . . .

"Drawing is, in all branches of industrial art, a means so evident, so useful, and so indispensable for embodying the conceptions of the mind, for studying and fixing the forms to be given to productions, for rendering the creative idea, that there can be no need of insisting on the necessity of developing that branch of instruction which has for its object the diffusion of such an acquirement among artisans of every class. This necessity, which has long been deeply felt in France, has led to the multiplication, in the great industrial centres, of schools for art and scientific drawing, which, while offering to the national taste the means of manifesting itself, have hitherto secured to French industry a great superiority in a large portion of its manufactures.

"The Universal Exhibition of 1855, and especially that of London in 1862, have clearly shown the results which England has already obtained from the immense efforts — among others the establishment of the splendid museum at Kensington — she has made, ever since 1852, to deprive France of that superiority in the works of industrial art, which the first exhibition of 1852 had proved to be indisputable. Soon after this exhibition, the most competent judges in England, far from refusing to acknowledge the pre-eminence of our artists over theirs, publicly proclaimed it; and, with the promptitude and active energy peculiar to their nation, they set about diffusing through all classes of society a taste for drawing and the arts, not only among working-men and artists, but also among the general public.

"The English Government, abandoning its principle of non-intervention in home administration, decided at this period on taking up the general organization of art education, and formed in the privy council, a new section under the name of 'Science and Art Department,' especially charged with propagating the study of drawing.

"The institutions dependent on the Science and Art Department are divided into two categories: —

"'1. *Public Teaching:* Schools of art and local associations of primary schools for teaching drawing; annual inspections of the local schools and primary schools combined in associations; annual local competitions; Central Museum at Kensington; loans of models and books on art from the museum to local schools; exhibition in the localities of the articles thus lent; pecuniary grants to the local schools for purchasing models, and, in certain cases, towards the expense of first establishment.

"'2. *Training of Art Masters:* Examinations of fitness, and graduated certificates; free admission of exhibitioners from the schools of art, and of pupil-teachers intended to become art-masters; normal school of art; certificates of fitness to teach elementary drawing, given upon examination to primary school-teachers of either sex.'

"Notwithstanding this organization, which would seem to indicate that the Art Department has become a sort of university for teaching drawing, acting like the French University for Literature and Science, the action of the department is limited to encouraging local or private foundations, to directing their efforts, to preparing and training capable teachers, and to indicating by general programmes the proper course to be followed.

"The summary programme of the central schools of drawing is as follows: —

"'1. *Elementary Course:* Geometrical drawing, linear perspective, free-hand drawing with shading, drawing from reliefs, figure-drawing from lithographed or engraved models, principle of water-color drawing.

"'2. *Superior Course:* Drawing from relief, painting, ornaments, flowers, still life, landscape.

"'3. *Special or Technical Course:* Art anatomy, elementary composition, designing, modelling, architectural and machine drawing.'

"MM. Marguérin and Mothéré's remarkable report, from which we have copied the above, contains very complete information respecting all this organization, which, in 1861, taught drawing to 91,836 pupils, more or less advanced.

"Everybody knows the magnificent Art Museum at South Kensington, for the founding of which the Science and Art Department has collected from all quarters masterpieces of every kind, at a total expense to the State of not less than a million pounds sterling since 1852. Besides this outlay for first establishment, the Art Department has a yearly grant of eighty thousand pounds sterling.

"By the extent of the resources placed at the disposal of this special and new department, created for the purpose of enabling English industry to compete with ours, an opinion may be formed of the importance rightly attributed in England to the participation of the art of design in all industrial productions. . . .

"England is not the only rival of French industry which has recognized its superiority with regard to works which require the aid of art and taste. Germany, moved by the same sentiment, has organized, since 1852, at less cost, but perhaps with as much success, drawing-schools of different degrees. In all the practical schools and in the polytechnic institutions, the teaching of drawing holds a prominent place. . . .

"The drawing-school which is justly regarded as the best in Central Germany is that of Nuremberg, the director of which has laid down the principle, that, to become a skilful industrial artist, it is indispensable first to study art in all its varieties. Under his energetic supervision a great number of professors and artists have been trained, who have disseminated good methods, and have brought about in the productions of industry, especially in those of Nuremberg, a most remarkable artistic improvement. . . .

"If the teaching of the art of drawing, considered as a whole, and with its principal varieties, should be regarded from a generally elevated point of view, even when the sole object is its application to the works of industry, it is advisable that the pupils should successively cultivate the higher branches, — the human figure, architecture, ornament, modelling, and sculpture on wood and stone; so that one and the same composition or subject may be conceived, treated, and executed by the same artist. To provide against the principal idea of a work being either weakened or entirely lost, the artist should be so far instructed in the different branches as not to be obliged, as some historical painters have been in times past, to get the architecture of their buildings drawn by one assistant, the landscape by a second, and sometimes the horses by a third. The history of the art and of the styles which have prevailed, and characterize the productions of different epochs, ought also to be the object of serious study; so that the artist may not be in danger of jumbling together in the same production the forms and ornaments belonging to very different periods and styles, as was the case with many of the English exhibitors in 1862. On this account, the demand for the founding of a superior school of industrial art, made in 1850 by the leading Parisian artists, appears to be well founded.

"Besides the study of artistic drawing, properly so called, that of linear drawing, based on geometrical principles, has also been widely extended in Germany. Descriptive geometry is taught elementarily, and with entirely practical applications, in the drawing-classes opened for artisans: there they also acquire the theory of projections. . . .

"Independently of the question of taste and art, which is of such vital importance for a great number of the higher branches of French industry, there is also a necessity, as many of the members of the commission have remarked, for introducing first into the primary schools, then into the technical classes of all kinds, the teaching and practice of geometrical drawing. This subject presents for the instruction of artisans the twofold advantage of giving the exact representation of the forms and proportions of objects, and the not less important one of supplying with the aid of models and simple apparatus, in a great number of cases, a direct means of demonstration. From this point of view, the teaching of geometrical drawing may be considered as a most effective auxiliary means in the method adopted for the technical instruction of workmen. Convinced of this truth, the commission expressed the following opinion : —

" 'The commission attaches great importance to extending the teaching of geometrical drawing as well in primary schools as in establishments devoted to technical instruction. It regards geometrical drawing as a most useful training for the practice of various trades, and as an excellent means of direct demonstration.' "

The English editor of the report, as printed by the English Government, adds a note to the following effect: —

" It may be remarked, however, that, in instruction in linear and machine drawing, we are much behind the countries of the Continent. It is not unusual to find in the drawing-offices of our great machine-works foreign draughtsmen. One of the reasons for this, no doubt, is the smaller rate of wages at which they can be obtained; but it seems, also, that the special instruction they have received in really scientific drawing gives them great advantage over the English draughtsman, who has studied his art only by rule of thumb. A reference to the table of the attendance at the government science classes will show, that, since the year 1864, the number of students attending the three drawing subjects — practical and descriptive geometry, machine construction and drawing, and building construction and drawing — has steadily and considerably increased. When practically and scientifically taught, the subject of descriptive geometry takes the place of mathematics in the technical training of those, who, from their limited elementary education, cannot appreciate the value of rigid mathematical proof, nor comprehend the use of formulæ."

The sub-commission of the French Imperial Commission, appointed to inquire into the state of technical instruction in Germany and Switzerland, say in their general report: —

"We may add as a general fact, that, in all kinds of technical instruction whatever, freehand and linear drawing rightly hold a prominent place; that they serve as a means of teaching by affording ocular demonstration of many matters which could scarcely be well understood by merely mental effort. As for the methods followed for this special teaching, that which — without exception, from the high school of Nuremberg to the humblest village classes in Wurtemberg — has always and everywhere been most successful is the one proposed by the late M. Dupuis, which has been too much neglected in France. It consists, as everybody knows, in making the pupils, either at the very outset, or after a few attempts at copying model drawings (to give freedom to the hand, and accustom it to act in accord with the eye), draw from subjects in relief: at first very simple, then combined and varied in position; rising gradually from subjects of ornaments in relief to drawing from the round or from nature. With a few unimportant modifications, this system is found in nearly all the schools of Germany. Persuaded as we are that one of the first and most important measures to be taken in organizing industrial education consists in teaching everywhere the art of drawing, we feel bound at once to call attention to the choice of this method."

In their special report on Austria, the sub-commission say:—

"Drawing is taught in the earliest classes from models in relief; and no copying is allowed, except for the purpose of teaching pupils to handle the pencil at the very outset. In the first year, the pupils of the first class, eleven years of age, practise freehand and elementary geometrical drawing, and make sketches of solid bodies and of geometrical forms, after models like those used in the Dupuis method. The use of rule and compasses is not permitted. They thus continue freehand drawings of ornaments from casts, make copies of heads, and finish by drawing from the round. In the third class, which contains pupils from thirteen to fifteen years of age, drawing receives considerable extension, especially with regard to its application to the practice of the trades the pupils intend to follow. With this view, special care is taken to make each pupil execute the designs which are most likely to be useful to him. For teaching descriptive geometry, much use is made of rectangular planes and pins, which render sensible to the eye all the rules of the projections. This, in fact, is the mode of teaching which has been proposed and employed by M. Olivier, professor at the Conservatory of Arts and Trades. His apparatus consists of two wooden planes articulated with hinges, and covered with cork, in which the pins are stuck to represent the lines of projection.

"The choice and number of the subjects treated in the three-years' studies are such that the young men who intend to follow the practical industries of constructing buildings or machines may obtain in the lower practical schools sufficient instruction to become master-builders, capable of understanding the plans to be executed, and of representing their own ideas in drawings. These lower schools are, therefore, well adapted for giving the pupils the theoretical instruction calculated to make them clever master-workmen, foremen, and conductors of works, when they shall have acquired the practical part of their trades in workshops and building-yards. The pupils who wish to continue their studies pass on to the fourth, fifth, and sixth classes, in which the teaching of drawing is at once theoretical and practical. . . .

"Of all the practical schools in Germany, that of Prague is certainly the one where linear drawing is best taught; and we are inclined to attribute this fact to the attention given from the very outset to the practice of freehand drawing, which early habituates the pupil to trace his lines with a light hand."

In their special report on Bavaria, the sub-commission say of Nuremberg: —

"In this town, so noted for its various manufactures, there are several drawing-schools of different degrees, according to the trade the pupils intend to follow. The first and most important is the higher school of industrial drawing conducted by M. Kröling. It is justly regarded in Germany as the one which has rendered most service to industry. In order that the pupils may, in a few years, acquire some real skill, none are admitted but those who have already attained considerable proficiency. The principle adopted by the professor of this school is, that, in order to form good industrial draughtsmen, the pupils must pass through all the degrees of artistic drawing; so that they may be able, in the very varied and different combinations required by manufacturers, to blend judiciously and harmoniously all the various kinds, without there being any necessity, as too often happens, for having recourse to one artist for the architectural part, to another for the figures, and to a third for the ornaments, &c.

"As for the method of teaching, it is exclusively based on drawing from models in relief, graduated according to the proficiency of the learners, and advancing from the simplest models to the finest left by ancient art, and then to nature. The talented director expresses his antipathy to copying from lithographs, which he regards as caligraphy, not drawing. In accordance with these principles, he has formed for his pupils very fine and very complete collections of models. The teaching is distributed in three divisions: 1. Drawing of ornament; 2. Drawing from the antique; 3. Drawing from nature. After attaining proficiency in drawing, the pupils pass on to modelling and sculpture in wood and stone: then, as soon as they have attained a certain degree of skill, they have to compose designs, and to model and carve them.

"The general opinion of the persons who have made a study of questions connected with teaching, not only in Bavaria, but also in other parts of Germany, is, that the Nuremberg school has contributed more than any other to the progress of the national industry. This progress is especially manifest in the very decided improvement in the manufacture of children's toys, which are one of the staple productions of the country. For some years past, the improvement in the forms of the articles, whether moulded in clay, or sculptured in wood, with which the Nuremberg manufacturers supply the shops of Paris, has shown us that great progress must have been made in the teaching of drawing; and ample confirmation of this opinion may be obtained on visiting the higher drawing-schools of this town. The Parisian manufacturers, though superior in other matters dependent on the arts of design, are, with regard to children's toys, very inferior to the Nuremberg artisans.

"As a preparation for the higher drawing-school, there is an elementary school, with courses occupying two years. The first, of eight hours per week, is entirely devoted to freehand drawing, beginning with exercises on straight lines and curves, on plane surfaces, on symmetrical and regular bodies, and on simplex and complex ornaments, finishing with compositions. The second course, of six hours per week, is devoted to drawing ornaments, to drawing from the round, from the antique, and also to drawing furniture."

In their special report on Wurtemberg, the sub-commission say: —

"One of the most remarkable features in the primary schools of Wurtemberg is the extraordinary attention paid to the teaching of drawing. The Department of Trade and Manufactures has persuaded the Ministry of Public Instruction and Worship to add classes for industrial drawing to all these schools; and the ministry has had the wisdom to leave to that department the care of organizing and superintending their progress. They were founded, after the Universal Exhibition of 1851, to enable the manufacturers of the country to compete with France in the industrial arts. These schools were at first gratuitous; but experience proved that attendance was better secured by requiring a small payment, varying, according to the means of parents, from half a florin to twelve florins a year.

"The teachers are, as far as possible, chosen from among the workmen or masters of the chief industries of the place, who, having been taught in the same schools, have there acquired the requisite knowledge. But these workmen thus made teachers do not abandon their trades, and receive only an indemnity of about two florins per hour's lesson. They generally give three a week, of two hours each, — from seven to nine o'clock in the evening. At Geisslingen, for instance, there is a school where a hundred and eighty scholars are taught by a master mason. In more than one parish the heads of establishments have so well appreciated the importance of this instruction, that they themselves send their young workmen and apprentices to the schools. It has been remarked that artists of considerable talent have not succeeded so well as masters, as mere artisans; which proves that there would not be so much difficulty as is supposed in expeditiously training teachers for this kind of schools.

"The Department of Trade has adopted examples to be used in all these schools, of which the first series, intended for beginners, consists of lithographs, easy, and few in number, merely for practice, — to give freedom to the hand while accustoming the pupil to guide it by the eye. The next step for the pupils is to draw from plaster models, graduated from the most simple figures to the finest casts from the antique, which are reserved for the principal schools. These models are supplied by an artist of Stuttgart, according to a tariff approved by the Department of Trade. They are delivered by him to the parish schools, which pay for them; but, at the end of the year, the department pays back to the schools one half the sum so disbursed. Besides these models in relief, the Department of Trade has formed a collection of the best publications on industrial art, from the most costly to the humblest albums of furniture, cabinet-work, bronzes, &c. It distributes these works throughout the country, lending them to the masters of the schools for a certain period, — usually one month. They must be returned in fair condition; and any damage suffered must be made good.

"Every other year, the schools send to Stuttgart a collection of their drawings of all kinds for exhibition; after which prizes are given to those which sent the finest productions. The masters themselves are invited to attend this exhibition, and to control the awards made. From among the most skilful masters a certain number are chosen, who during the vacation, or at other times, go round to the schools as occasional inspectors, and suggest improvements to the masters; sometimes even giving them private lessons.

"Drawing also forms part of the instruction given in the normal school for primary teachers; so that they may be able thereafter to teach their pupils the first elements. A few of the pupils who have shown most skill and taste are sent to the Superior Art School at Nuremberg.

"Thus there have been established in the kingdom of Wurtemberg more than four hundred drawing-schools; and this organization, which does not date back more than ten years, has already led to very decided improvements in the manufactures of the country.

"It is satisfactory to know that the designers trained in these schools, if they evince any considerable degree of taste and invention, easily find occupation in their own country. The more distinguished among them are sometimes sent to France for improvement. Great emulation exists among the teachers and professors of drawing; and, besides the biennial exhibitions made by order of the government, an association has been formed by the masters, which, aided by voluntary contributions, has raised a fund for the purpose of organizing regular exhibitions of all the pupils' drawings, and for awarding prizes."

The Imperial Commission, in their summary of the Inquiry on Professional Education, say: —

"Among all the branches of instruction, which in different degrees, from the highest to the lowest grade, can contribute to the technical education of either sex, *drawing, in all its forms and applications, has been almost unanimously regarded as the one which it is most important to make common.*"

REPLIES TO LORD STANLEY'S CIRCULAR.

[See Chap. II. for the particulars about Lord Stanley's circular letter.]

Mr. Ward, answering from Hamburg (Germany), says, giving the director of the Hamburg Trade School as authority: —

"Free drawing without instruments begins with drawing from wooden models, according to Heimerdinger's method, in which simple objects, such as tools used by joiners, engineers, &c., are included; attention being paid to the vocation of the pupil in the choice of the models. Ornamental drawing from plaster casts, in outline, and in respect to shading, then follows. Those pupils who devote themselves to building or ornamental trades study the figure from casts and anatomy. The metal-workers draw freely, without instruments, portions of machinery, &c. The mode of execution (which is with lead-pencil, pen, brush, and rubber) is always the most suitable to the branch of technical art to which the pupil intends to devote himself. In close connection with this style of drawing are the exercises in ornamental design. Plants, flowers, and leaves are drawn from life; and these drawings are used in designing. By these exercises the pupils become very soon independent of all help. Geometrical drawings are executed from large copies. The teachers explain the perfect principles of construction, and pay special attention to exactness in execution. When the pupil has acquired confidence in the use of his instruments, and has mastered the essential principles, the measuring and drawing of some simple and more complicated bodies follows. This class is attended by metal-workers, joiners, builders and carpenters, carriage-builders, ship-builders, &c. The instruction is imparted by measuring and drawing real objects, such as parts of machinery, tools, furniture, doors, windows, carriages, &c., according to fixed rules and specified plans.

"Instruction in freehand drawing can only be of use to the pupils when they use real objects, and not drawings. By the method pursued here, the hand needs no particular preparation, because the nearest model offers an example by which the hand and eye are both alike exercised. No particular introduction to the rules of perspective is needed. The scholar learns to see correctly; and his attention is directed to the principles of perspective by the teacher.

"From the specimens of freehand drawing which were exhibited at Paris this year, it would appear that no method can compare with that here referred to, for producing a satisfactory result in a short time. The results of several other industrial schools are in this respect far behind those of the Hamburg School. Drawing from specimens should be entirely avoided in industrial schools, in freehand as well as in geometrical and technical drawing. . . .

"In all these trade schools (at Frankfort-on-the-Main) the greatest value is always placed upon the instruction in drawing. Freehand drawing is begun from the flat, and goes on, as soon as possible, to drawing from the round and from plaster casts; in which particular regard is paid to ornament. Even with the more advanced pupils, less regard is paid to shading and the formation of shadows than to the outline. Only the best pupils are occasionally allowed to undertake shading, and then only with the stump.

"Linear drawing is, as a rule, begun with the construction of geometric figures, by which the pupil is practised in the use of the rule, the compass, and the drawing-pen: he then proceeds to the copying of simple implements, to which succeeds drawing from wooden models, and, lastly, exercises in construction.

"The descriptive geometry as taught at Stuttgart and Nuremberg is very profitable for various trades, — such as workers in tin, bookbinders, &c., — as the pupils are taught the drawing of network, the intersection of plane surfaces, &c. With linear drawing it might be advisable, as far as possible, to divide it according to industries, especially in the higher branches."

From Paris Lord Lyons sends, among other things, the methods prescribed by the government for instruction in the special schools. With reference to descriptive geometry, which is the basis of so much mechanical drawing, it is directed: —

"Many pupils find it difficult to represent to themselves the geometric figures in space, to read in space, as it is called: nevertheless, to read in space is an indispensable faculty for artisans and other persons following industrial pursuits; and every effort must be made to develop it in the pupils of the special schools. The teachers of descriptive geometry should, therefore, make use of the planes with turning joints, and the stems furnished with points, which are used in the *Conservatoire des Arts et Métiers,* in order to represent straight lines and planes, and to render palpable their various respective positions. The pupils — being provided with similar apparatus, but on a smaller scale — should themselves realize the figures proposed. When all the pupils have finished their constructions, the professor should exhibit his from every point of view, in order to accustom the eyes of the pupils to the different aspects under which it may appear: finally, suppressing lines and planes, he should draw on the board the material figure which he has just constructed, after having assured himself that all the pupils have read correctly in space, and have understood the relations of the lines and the planes. The instruction given in this way is slower; but it keeps alive the attention of the young people. The method is, besides, indispensable for many of them. The success of the pupils in the study of projections, perspective, and cosmography, and as regards the works which they will one day have to undertake, depends entirely on their perfect understanding of this first part of the course; which is, as it were, the alphabet of a more complex kind of reading.

"It is well known that the data of a practical geometrical question are essentially numerical: thus a point is given by the distances of the two planes of projection, measured and expressed in metres and centimetres; a straight line, by two of its numbered points, and, frequently, by a point and the angles which the straight line makes with the planes of projection, &c. The pupils should, therefore, be early exercised in constructing on some given scale the data of the question proposed. The amplifications, the reductions, the changes of scale, ought to be rendered familiar to them by numerous examples. Every problem in the theory has its correspondent in numerical data; and all the plans are executed on a given scale. Furthermore, as the instruction is addressed to young people, who, as yet, are little accustomed to abstract considerations, their eyes ought to be constantly appealed to in aid of their understanding. The professor should, therefore, propose numerous examples in support of the principles propounded; and the objects in relief should be placed before the pupils. The representation of bodies should be much dwelt upon. The proposed exercises are, in the first place, useful in themselves, because they give to the pupils their first notions of frame-work (*charpente*); but the exercises are more especially beneficial by giving the pupils the habit of reading the language of projections, and of figuring to themselves objects in space. Lastly, every opportunity should be seized for representing simple applications to stone-cutting and the determination of shadows: —

"Representation of a point and a straight line to trace the projection of a cube, a prism, a pyramid; some simple joinings of timber-work, such as joining with mortise and tenons, &c.; projections of a pair of principals; representation of a plane, straight lines (*droites*), and perpendicular planes; method of rabbeting(*rabattements*), angle of two straights; angles of two planes; rotatory movement round a vertical axis; applications; intersections of a sphere and a plane; curve of contact of a sphere with a circumscribed cylinder," &c.

TESTIMONY OF ENGLISH ARTISANS.

[See Chap. II. for particulars about the report of the English artisans who were sent to the Paris Exhibition in 1867.]

Benjamin Lucraft, chair-maker, says: —

"Having on other occasions, when in Paris, observed that lads of fourteen or fifteen years of age were intrusted with superior work to that of our lads in London, I determined to make the subject one of special inquiry; and, while visiting one of the factories already named, a good opportunity offered. Seeing some lads at work with the men in the carvers' shop, I went to the bench of one about fourteen. He was carving a chair-back of a mediæval pattern, from a working-drawing: it was nearly finished, and well carved. Finding, from inquiry, that he had done the whole himself, I expressed my surprise that one so young was found capable of carving so well, and was informed that boys at school are specially prepared for the trade they fancy, or that their friends have decided upon for them; so that a boy about to be apprenticed to learn carving is instructed in ornamental drawing, modelling, and designing."

Francis Kirchoff, glass-painter, reports: —

"The French work, when compared with the English, shows a greater diversity of design in construction, and more freedom and grace in the drawing of the ornament; but, in excellence of color and pleasing harmony, the English glass is much superior."

In his report, James Mackie, wood-carver, says: —

"I visited the *École Impériale Speciale pour l'Application des*

Beaux Arts à l'Industrie. On that occasion there was an exhibition of the works of the students; and the number and variety were considerable and interesting. Conspicuous among the exhibits were some large models in clay. The minister of instruction had dictated the subject; and the following were the particulars given: A somewhat large tympanum of a pediment, to have the head of a bull for the centre, resting upon a shield, with accessories of boys, and festoons of fruit and flowers. The best was a very successful interpretation of the order given. A vase, intended to be executed in silver, was also modelled according to instructions. There were several competitors in each case. These studies were little more than good sketches in clay; but it was evident that the students were learning a most useful lesson, that would stand them in good service when they went forth into the world. There were the usual school studies, both in clay modelling and drawing, or rather superior sketching; the prettiness and high finish aimed at in the English schools being left alone. There were copies of casts of figures and ornament, drawings of natural leaves and flowers, sketches (from memory) of well-known works, original designs, and sketches done in a given time. All of them were interesting, and indicated great industry and a promise of excellence. It seemed abundantly clear that the system pursued was simple and rapid, and that the teaching and practice produced valuable results. It seems to have great vitality; never being without deep and varied interest to the students, — features that should distinguish every school, and without which they will assuredly fail in accomplishing the objects sought to be attained. This system of being content with good sketching in all branches of instruction in art seems to be the life and soul of art as applied to maufactures. Good sketching is acquired; and, as few will require to gain a subsistence by making finished pictures, a valuable and sufficient power is gained that is always in great request, and is never lost.

"A visit to the exhibition of the works of the students of the *École Impériale Speciale de Dessin pour les Jeunes Personnes* showed that the young ladies practised the same system with very profitable results, although in a less degree. Their studies partook largely of pen-and-ink drawings, with a view to the practice of the art of wood-engraving."

R. Baker, wood-carver, reports: —

"A knowledge of drawing being essential to a good carver, the schools of design in Paris are more numerous, and easier of access, than in London. Their system of teaching is superior for practical purposes to our own: it gives a better general idea of the object designed. Instead of exact outline, and a slow and tedious process of shading, they time their pupils, allow them more latitude, and get a better general resemblance of the object copied. Apprentices generally attend these schools in the evening. At the age of thirteen or fourteen, boys are apprenticed, serving three to five years, and are remunerated in proportion to what they earn. This encourages quickness. Being free at the age of seventeen or eighteen, they change their workshops, and gain experience, at the age when the mind is best suited for receiving instruction. At twenty-one he is already an experienced workman, just when our apprentices are merging from their semi-torpid existence."

William Letheren, art-metal workman, says: —

"The skill of the smith is displayed in uniting the parts of a piece of iron-work, so that the different leaves and other parts, when completed, form a whole, blending one with the other. Then we get use, durability, and ornament combined. This the older smiths made their study; and it should be our aim to excel them. In this class of work, the workman must not only be practical, but have a knowledge of design and drawing. In this, as a rule, the English workmen are behind: for we may find many a good smith; but, having no knowledge of drawing, he only destroys the good effect intended by the designer.

"I think the schools of art have done much toward the improvement of the mechanic; but few avail themselves of the opportunity. The French have an advantage in this respect; the master of an apprentice is bound by law to give him two hours a day for education: and the class of schools formed for such have a peculiar advantage, inasmuch as the artisan is invited to bring specimens of work of whatever kind; and prizes are awarded, at certain times, to those that excel. In this respect the French are far before the English."

In his special report on the condition and habits of the French working-classes, Richard Whiteing says: —

"We are convinced a course of systematic instruction in the principles of design, and the nature of materials, is what is most needed in our art schools at the present day. It is not enough to give men the best examples to copy, the best materials to use: the greatest care should be taken to explain to them why those examples and those materials are considered the best; to show them that beauty in the wrong place becomes deformity; and how narrow is the boundary line, which in art, as indeed in every field of human endeavor, separates the sublime from the ridiculous. All, or nearly all, the faults which in the past were charged against

English design, were mainly traceable to the causes we have pointed out. It was not denied that there was beauty here and there in our houses, our furniture, our dress; but what was complained of was, that those beauties were mostly chosen without any perception of harmony in their relation the one to the other. They were exotics from many climes, loosely jumbled together, each neutralizing the effect of the other. Since the establishment of art schools in this country, we have made a much nearer approach to congruity of ornament; but much yet remains to be done: whereas, in the earliest examples of French manufacture, there is always visible a certain sense of the becoming, a certain harmony of parts, and subjugation of details to one leading idea, — a false one it may be, but still having a distinct individuality of its own. The word 'style' is always on the French workman's lips; and its claims are no less rigorously enforced in the inferior products of the industry of our neighbors than in their highest efforts in literature and in art."

James Taylor, practical foreman of gas-fittings manufactory, Birmingham, says: —

"With respect to education, I did not have an opportunity to notice much more than that the workpeople generally are much better up in fine arts than our people. This I think a great failing with the English, — that they are not sufficiently educated in drawing and the fine arts. I think, unless there is something done in this direction, that we shall not retain the supremacy we now hold with respect to the chandelier trade. France has made such progress in the trade these last few years, that, unless something is done in that direction, we shall not be able to keep pace with the French."

William Gorman, brass-founder, says: —

"Taking our own productions in this branch generally, our great deficiency is in design, in which we are surpassed by most of the nations on the Continent: and the deficiency is not confined to ornamental articles; for the plain are frequently very bad in form. I believe one great cause of this defect to be the custom which generally prevails of employing the workman to make his own patterns. If we are to maintain our position, we must pay more attention to form and design, and encourage education in this important direction."

James Plampin, working-jeweller, reports: —

"Their superiority is in taste; and taste is essentially a matter of education. Owing to the extent of this kind of education, the taste of the *whole nation* is higher than that of the English. While, perhaps, there are scarcely more than four out of two hundred English jewellers that can draw, from inquiries made there are scarcely four out of two hundred in France who cannot. Nor is this surprising, when we learn that drawing is regarded and taught more as an essential than as an accomplishment. As children, they are taught at the day-school, and that not occasionally, but as part of the usual routine."

Frank J. Jackson, designer and art teacher from Birmingham, says, in his report of the Paris Exhibition: —

"One noticeable feature in French industry is the universal application of art, no object being too mean for adornment; and every article capable of being turned into a thing of beauty receives its share of attention at the hands of the artist. To such an extent is this love of art carried, that mere mechanical finish is sacrificed at the shrine of beauty; and we find that the very things we pride ourselves upon, and boast of achieving, are by them set at nought in favor of aiming at a higher quality. In England I find the matter is entirely different. Where there is an attempt to develop a better style of art, it is almost sure to be of a special and restrictive character; and it invariably occurs that the same house that will produce rare and costly works fails to devote that attention to ordinary wares, so as to raise their artistic character; being content with ugliness, so long as the objects are perfect in polish, and have passed through the routine of processes that are ever dear to the mechanical mind. Again: the vitality of French art is very remarkable. In their search after novelty, they show a wholesome disregard for that which has gone before, and strike out with an amount of artistic daring that is startling, yet, nevertheless, governed by such taste, that their very extravagances pass unchallenged, and surprise us into admiration. Their treatment of the human figure is, perhaps, of a more daring character than even their use of ornament, both of which are rendered with great warmth and brilliancy, — qualities which are never neglected, whatever style of decoration they may adopt. For example, the style now so much in use is the Greek; but instead of its being the cold, severe style of the past, in their hands it becomes revivified, rivalling their favorite *renaissance*, and earning the name justly bestowed of 'Neo Grec.' . . .

"The facilities for French students of industrial art are very great. Besides the ordinary academies, they have what are called 'technical schools,' where, in the same institution, drawing is taught, in which a knowledge of a trade to which art is to be applied can also be acquired, the fees for which are almost nominal. This class of school is, I think, of the utmost value, and clearly demonstrates that the French do really possess 'schools of practical art.' The system of drawing pursued, as far as I could judge from an examination of many folios of drawings shown in the Exhibition, is very excellent. There seems to be no over-anxiety for fineness of outline; while in shading, the readiest method is generally adopted, more importance being attached to the realization of form, and less to mere manipulation. Great stress also seems to be laid upon drawing from the human figure, and flowers from nature. Most of the specimens I saw were very spiritedly executed, but scarcely up to the English notion of neatness. The method of teaching carried on in our government schools offers a marked contrast to that of the French. Examine the drawings that are occasionally exhibited, and it will be found that an immense amount of labor is spent upon fineness of line and mechanical finish. In this respect, I think we are decidedly in error; in fact, we begin at the wrong end. Fineness and neatness of line are the results of much practice, and in early training are of much less importance than the acquisition of correct notions of size, proportions, and forms: to insist too strongly on the former is to jeopardize the realization of the latter. Again: I do not think we have sufficient drawing from nature, from the human figure, or flowers; and much of the students' time that is spent in making copies from the 'flat' would be more effectually employed in drawing from *objects*. Drawing from the 'flat' is only the beginning of the end: whereas it too generally appears as if copying was the end itself. Still further, we are entirely without any institutions, that I am aware of, that will compare with the French technical schools, the importance of which can scarcely be overrated. Our schools of design are not at all comparable with them; for they give no evidence of a special course of instruction any more than is shown by ordinary private academies."

Mr. James Hole, honorable secretary of the Yorkshire Union of Mechanics' Institutes, in a letter in 1868 to Lord Montagu, vice-president of the Committee of Council on Education, says: —

"Our art schools do not bear a sufficiently close relation to the actual work in which art workmen are engaged to give the latter a personal interest in the studies. The great merit of the trade schools on the Continent is the intimate relation they establish between the instruction in science and art, and its practical applications. Our schools of art produce highly-elaborated works, much as if we aimed at producing artists rather than skilled workmen. The national medals are given for excellence in subjects interesting mainly to amateurs, artists, and professional teachers, — painting from nature in colors, drawing from the antique, and design, — but in which manufacturers and machinists have little share, as medals are not given for excellence in mechanical drawing. No examples for students to draw from are provided for the schools of art; and those that are made use of in the Leeds School of Art (the centre of a machine-making district) are French drawings purchased in Paris.

"Until the instruction of the schools can be made to have a more direct bearing upon industrial work, neither workingmen nor their employers can be expected to take a very strong interest in the schools. But once establish that relation, and it probably would not be difficult to induce employers to permit a small portion of the work-time to be devoted to the purpose of practically illustrated brief lectures on the principles involved in their work. And, if the employers were thus enabled to see the importance of this union of knowledge with labor, artisans would likewise deem it an object of ambition; and we should thus get some of the best results of the Continental trade schools. It is vain to expect that any considerable portion of our workmen will give up their hardly-earned leisure for studies the importance of which they cannot yet feel. During the recent discussions on this subject at Birmingham, a manufacturer stated that he had introduced lessons on design into his workshop for the benefit of his apprentices, and with the most beneficial and satisfactory results."

TESTIMONY OF SCOTT RUSSELL.

Mr. J. Scott Russell, in his work on the "Systematic Technical Education of the English People," says: —

"It is not enough that the workman thoroughly masters the form which his work shall take: he must also be able to draw what we have called the three plans of his work on paper. This may be considered an unnecessary piece of skill for the man who has only to do the particular work assigned to him, and of which, probably, a perfect pattern is put before his eyes to guide him. But the mere seeing of his pattern is not adequate to superior execution. Every bit of work which one man does has to fit into some other bit of work of some other man's doing. In work there are degrees, — perfect fit and misfit of all grades. To make his work fit other people's, a man must know, not merely his own, but that of all about him. Each man should therefore understand the plans of the complete work on which he and his fellows are engaged, in order to work well to the other's hand. The only way to get this thorough understanding of plans is to have learned to draw them one's self. Complete plan-drawing, applied to his own business, is therefore essential to a good workman."

It was generally conceded by the artists of England, and by foreign visitors, that the textile manufactures from India were the most perfect in design of any that appeared in the London Exhibition, 1851. Owen Jones, the author of "The Grammar of Ornament," referring to this fact, says, "We see in the ornaments and articles from India the works of a people who are not allowed by their religion to draw the human form; and it is probable, that to this cause we may attribute their great success in their ornamental works. Here in Europe we have been studying drawing from the human figure; but it has not led us forward in the art of ornamental design. Although the study of the human figure is useful in refining the taste, and teaching accurate observation, it is a roundabout way of learning to draw for the designer for manufactures."

A simple glance at the programme of any special school for industrial education, even for agriculture or gardening, will show how much importance is attached to drawing in nearly all parts of Europe. Thus about one-half of the time, on an average, is devoted to drawing in all the trade schools of Germany; which schools are for the instruction of apprentices and master artisans. In the lower practical schools, not designed for any particular industry, from two to four hours a week are consumed in drawing; while, in the higher practical schools, drawing occupies from one-quarter to one-third of the time. In the technical universities and colleges, the students give about one-half of their time to drawing. Some, of course, give more, some less, according to the department of industry for which they are preparing. What is true of Germany is true of France, of Switzerland, and of other European countries. Then below all this lies that earlier instruction in drawing which is almost universally given in the elementary schools, where the education of the whole people begins.

BELGIAN TESTIMONY.

A congress to examine into the best methods of making artistic instruction general was held at Brussels, Sept. 21–23, 1868. This congress was attended by a large number of teachers and inspectors of drawing from the Belgian academies, by Belgian painters and sculptors, and by delegates from various foreign countries. In his opening address, defining the object of the congress, the questions to be discussed, M. Visschers, member of the Board of Mines, and president of the Committee of Organization, said:—

"GENTLEMEN,—You have all seen the remarkable exposition of drawings by the pupils of our academies and our free schools. A jury, composed of competent men, has been commissioned to judge of these productions, and to propose to the government the distribution of suitable rewards, to be given to the authors of the best works. Our duty, on the other hand, will be to examine the questions contained in our programme,—'the extension of the instruction in the principles of drawing to all the primary schools, and re-organization of the artistic instruction imparted in the secondary and higher schools.' The subject before us to-day is inseparably interwoven with the true interests of the mass of the people, the advancement of industry, the useful and the fine arts. The question is, by what means we can place in the hands of all men, particularly the working-man and mechanic, a new instrument to increase their personal capital,—the power of usefulness and enjoyment."

As with other educational subjects, the discussion which followed developed a variety of opinions, more or less divergent, as to the best manner of teaching drawing. It was generally agreed, however, that drawing ought to be introduced into all the primary schools, and should consist chiefly of linear drawing.

M. Von Marke said he would begin with straight

lines, then proceed to geometrical figures, followed by rectilinear designs, and then by those having curved lines, advancing to ornaments. The pupil could now take up drawing from nature with advantage, copying solids first, then models of simple ornament, gradually advancing to things more elaborate and difficult.

Having been urged by many members of the congress, M. Hendricks, whose method of teaching drawing has been widely commended in Europe, described it, in brief, thus: —

MISTAKEN STUDY OF THE HUMAN FIGURE.

"I must state here, that I had investigated every thing carefully before I became aware of the evil (the deplorable state of instruction in drawing in its application to industry and the different trades), and found that it consisted alone in confused ideas on the part of teachers. In my opinion, this evil is not the consequence of want of talent in those who teach: on the contrary, many of our teachers are very competent; and by far the greater number possess undoubted talent. No: the fault lies in another direction, — in that too frequent and widespread mistake, that the study of the human figure suffices, and ought to precede every thing else, how inferior soever the trade may be to which the pupil intends to devote himself. There lies the mistake, and the generally-acknowledged decline of our artistic teaching in its applications to the various branches of our national labor. I will prove this by mentioning a few simple statistics. Upwards of ten thousand pupils attend annually our various academies and schools of design;

and the majority of them have practised nothing but copying the human figure from engravings or plaster casts. Now, if this exclusive study was sufficient, ought not our manufactures, as a general rule, to show the highest artistic taste? We all know that this is far from being the case. Nobody will deny that the study of the human figure is the basis of all purely artistic teaching. But it may likewise be very justly remarked, that several branches of art — such as the painting of landscapes, flowers, views of cities, naval scenes, and many other subjects — have been cultivated to their highest degree of perfection, without their authors being able to show a profound knowledge of the study of the human figure. A great number of other less important branches of art may likewise thrive without having this study for their basis. To the decorator or ornamental sculptor, the natural kingdoms furnish a large number of other elements which are just as indispensable for him. The foundation of his whole art lies, more than anywhere else, in the study of the various phenomena presented by the vegetable kingdom, from whose inexhaustible sources, he, from time immemorial, has drawn the ideas for his most beautiful creations, and his happiest applications to useful objects, as well as for the architectural designs which antiquity has bequeathed to us.

GEOMETRY THE TRUE BASIS OF ALL ELEMENTRY DRAWING.

"According to my idea, all elementary drawing should take, as its foundation, geometry, and make the elements of this science subservient to the analysis of artistic forms, in such a manner that they are not an inanimate instrument only, but, on the contrary, a means by which the pupil can himself control and appreciate his work. Every method should be rational, positive, and not leave room for doubt in the pupil's mind. This is the idea which has served me as a starting-point in making out the method which I am about to lay before you. I have arranged it in such a manner that the pupil is at once enabled to appreciate the peculiarities of the most complicated forms, using simpler forms with which he has already been made familiar.

FIRST DEGREE OF TEACHING.

"*These studies consist in the free-hand drawing of forms and figures, in general, geometrically represented.* Before letting the pupil reproduce a copy of the smallest object, we exercise his eyes and his hands in using elementary figures which allow him to understand gradually their relative proportions, their characteristic combination, their particular form, and, finally, all their details. On the thorough practice of these preliminary exercises depend the immediate and complete results in the reproduction of forms and figures. The pupil, knowing how to construct (by free-hand drawing) a perfect square, and rectangular figures of all dimensions, will gradually apply the generic geometrical figures which he has been taught. This knowledge, practically acquired, will enable him to understand immediately the characteristic combination of the object presented to him, to analyze all its outlines, and reproduce them in all their relative dimensions.

SECOND DEGREE OF TEACHING.

"*Solids, their Construction and their Study.* — As in the first degree of teaching, we also here, before letting the pupil copy from some figure, give him the means of understanding the form, and the way in which it is composed. We commence by making him understand the construction of elementary figures. He learns, first of all, the construction of the cube, and its different rectangular divisions, and, next, to place it in all the positions possible. If he has once acquired this foundation, he successively refers to it all the generic forms, the combinations of which he makes in the various positions which the teacher prescribes. He proves by this that he can see in the space, and that he possesses a correct knowledge of the principal parts of which any given figure is composed. Arrived at this point of his studies, he undertakes the construction of more developed figures, at the same time studying the various elements of ornaments in their second degree. He represents, on an even surface, what a moulder represents by his mould. He sees solid forms; and he will soon be able to express his thoughts in drawing, building, &c., forms which constitute the object of his special study.

THIRD DEGREE OF TEACHING.

"*Drawing after Objects or Figures placed at some Distance.* — It is indispensable here, that, at the very outset, the pupil should become thoroughly familiar with the rules of perspective; but, simple and easy as they are in their application to the whole figure, just as difficult and tedious do they become in their regular application to the construction of every single part of an object. In recommending the study of the rules of this science, we do not mean the rigorous application of these rules to the elevations on the profiles of the thousand different points of a capital (of a pillar) or other architectural ornaments. We will leave this to men who study science for its own sake. What we want is this: that the pupil learn to know the construction of the objects which he has to represent, that then he may learn to give to all the details of this object their proper perspective position. The same would also apply to the study of light and shade.

"Any pupil who is in earnest, and has thus been prepared by the elementary and analytical study of the three degrees of our method, will be able in less than a year to copy any object placed before him, and do it successfully. Thus does the first degree comprise the study of forms geometrically represented, and the means of reproducing them in all their just proportions; whilst the second and third degrees have for their aim the initiation of the pupil in the construction and reproduction of forms and figures such as they present themselves in space."

M. de Taeye, Director of the Royal Academy of Fine Arts at Louvain, said: —

"We may here, for safety, establish this principle: the elementary study of every kind of drawing must be based on geometrical forms; only we shall see, that, in putting it into practice, it is indispensable to pursue two different ways. By geometrical drawing, one arrives at an exact, precise, and mathematical representation of the object, taking note of its length, breadth, &c. Thus the mind gets a complete knowledge of its real form, and is enabled to make the most delicate analysis; whilst, by drawing from sight, one only takes note of the apparent form of the object, according to the point of view from which one considers it, without being able to arrive at an analysis of its real form. The first way of drawing obtains its results by means of instruments, such as ruler and compasses; whilst the second relies substantially on the exercise of the eye, and the practice of the hand. I believe, therefore, that a combination of these two methods is an absolute necessity in order to constitute a complete and rational system of teaching which satisfies the demands of imagination and reason."

[For a fuller account of the discussion by the congress at Brussels, see "Technical Education," by Henry Barnard, LL.D.]

FRENCH REPORT ON DRAWING, AT THE UNIVERSAL EXPOSITION, PARIS, 1867.

The following is the report made to the French Minister of Public Instruction, by the committee on "instruction in drawing in the normal schools, the primary schools, and the course for adults," in France: —

"Commissioned by your Excellency to examine the drawings executed for the Universal Exposition, we finished the first part of this work with M. Brongniart, inspector of schools for the city of Paris, placing a mark upon each drawing to indicate its value.

"My colleague of the superior council of special instruction, M. Sebastien Cornu, desired to repeat the examination with me; and we have ranked each of the schools whose products were displayed at the Exposition.

"We have, therefore, had a double means of verification, of proof, in an investigation which we wished to make with extreme care, as we desired to respond the best we could to the felicitous thought which your Excellency has expressed for the improvement of drawing in France.

"We realize the full importance of your resolves concerning this matter, now that we have seen the sacrifices made abroad, especially in England and Germany, in order to enter the pathway of a like progress.

"Hitherto, relying on an honorable past, on great examples, and on this personal initiative, which have been regarded wrongly, according to our view, as sufficient in art, things have, in large measure, been left to themselves in France. Undoubtedly, even without direction, without schools, without encouragement, there will always arise on French soil, artists, — choice natures, — who will leave the multitude in spite of every thing; but if the times, if the conditions, become little favorable, these happy exceptions will be more rare: some natural dispositions will be smothered, others perverted. Genius itself, without severe study, shrinks to the proportions of talent. An age will give Watteau or Boucher in place of Leonardo da Vinci and Louini. *And, if we go back to the real influences which determine the merit of artists, we see of what necessity are classic studies from the very dawn of life; indeed, how the first instruction in drawing is responsible for the future public taste.*

"It is of this future we would wish to speak with entire freedom.

"Present results, so far as relates to mechanical drawing, graphic drawing, machine-drawing, are almost always very satisfactory: on the contrary, when we consider ornamentation, the copies and models and the instruction are equally defective; while all that pertains to the figure, to imitation-drawing, is worse still.

"If we except the schools of Paris, Potiers, Nancy, Mulhouse, Metz, Grenoble, Orléans, St. Quentin, Rochefort, the normal schools of Tulle, Chaumont, Cluny, the lay schools of Beauvais, d'Épinal, Péronne, Chapelle-sur-Loir, the ecclesiastic schools of Mézières, Sedan, Bayeux, Rive-de-Gier, and Reims, the specimens, the works of the pupils which we have had in hand, show how much good a prompt reform would do. In the normal schools, in the imperial lyceums, — that is to say, in the schools for the class called to direct, to form, to elevate others, — we have found the drawings much inferior to those which a school of workmen in Paris could execute. It seems to us important that this should not be so. Out of Paris, in the matter of drawing, there is, with very rare exceptions, no su periority manifested by the adult classes or in the popular courses. There is almost everywhere an equally bad level. Yet we have often found among the pupils a great desire to do well, real aptitude, with an enormous amount of work.

"As far as we can see, with some remarkable exceptions, the time devoted to imitation-drawing is almost completely lost; and these are the principal causes of this misfortune : —

"Everywhere the copies and models of figures and of ornaments are as bad as possible, and will be the cause of perpetuating bad taste and ignorance. Many of the teachers of drawing, who have often been the first victims of this state of things, cannot draw : what is worse, they do not know how the drawing should be done; while their taste is that of the copies and models which they buy. They teach error with a profound conviction, with the best possible faith. The notes placed by them upon the miserable productions of patience very badly employed often showed, that, if the master did not do the work for his pupil, he was ready to indorse it.

"Another cause of evil is this : in the lyceums, in the colleges, the drawing-lesson, taken out of the time for recreation, has always been considered by the students as a species of encroachment upon their rest and their sports. They come, therefore, to these studies, however attractive in themselves, with an ill-humor which they regard as well founded. They are resolved on a retaliation, of which they are the first dupes in reality, and defend themselves against the lesson, instead of seeking to profit by it as do the pupils in the artisan classes. Those only, and at the last moment, who are going to the special schools, strive to learn just that which they regard as sufficient to cover their ignorance, and help them through their examination.

"Finally, there is a graver cause than bad instruction : it is found in the debasement of the public taste. This is sometimes a species of weakening of the moral sense, revealed by certain lamentable signs.

THE GREAT VALUE OF GOOD DRAWING-COPIES.

"When we have striven to discover what is best in France, in order to ask your Excellency how to make it general by searching for that which had produced it, my colleagues and myself have been surprised to see how the art sentiment, perceptible even in the drawings of children (if we may speak of them), is radically modified by the objects which are constantly under the eyes. I desire to mention only one striking example.

"The city of Nancy sent landscapes, figures, ornaments, flowers, executed by different schools. In spite of the variety of instruction, all the works had a unique character of grandeur, of amplitude, a little marred, however, by that bad taste which Stanislas everywhere impressed upon a city rebuilt in one period. The influence of that period — of that architecture of Stanislas — has been such that we can recognize a drawing from Nancy among a thousand.

"The models, therefore, are not simply those sheets of paper which are only for an hour under the eyes during the drawing-lesson, but every thing, indeed, which we behold in childhood; especially every thing which we regard with passion, with love.

"Thus at Athens, when the Greek chisels cut the marble, they could produce only beautiful things. Doubtless, it is impossible to give the children of a little town, otherwise than by photography and engraving, specimens of beautiful monuments capable of enlarging, elevating, their ideas. But, if one cannot always procure the best, to shun bad impressions is a duty.

"After this assault upon bad drawings, we shall ask you to have excellent ones made; for this is the true way to fortify against the bad. We could wish to see appear a complete, serviceable series of figures, ornaments, flowers. Beyond the good ones which already exist, would it not be possible to obtain some contributions from certain large commercial cities, or from establishments having a direct interest in the creation of schools of taste, of schools of practical and serious art? Would it not be possible to imitate the great progress accomplished in Paris?

WHAT PARIS HAS DONE FOR DRAWING IN THE MUNICIPAL SCHOOLS.

"I would like here to give the provinces an account of what the city has done—I ought to say, grandly, generously—with such far-seeing liberality. I wish the inspectors of the departments could see what I began to examine first as a matter of conscience, of duty, but which I afterwards studied with extreme interest,—the schools of drawing, the schools for adults in Paris.

"A few years ago the city authorities perceived how important it was, at this juncture of affairs of industry, to have at its service more artisans who understood drawing,—men of taste in all the departments of labor. Embossers, sculptors, metal-workers, those who produce pottery, objects of luxury, all have need of artistic studies, which make the worth of the man, the worth of the article, and the fortune of the merchant.

"And yet Paris had for schools only certain miserable low halls, without air, windows narrow, badly lighted by day, badly lighted also by night; and what copies! what models! But in spite of this, in spite of the insufficient appointments, so deleterious to the health of the pupils, so little attractive to young men, for whom every thing around them was attractive, these miserable schools were full. Stone-cutters wished to become sculptors; at least in the next generation. House-painters aspired to become decorators. Knowledge of personal interest recommended the study of art, for the purpose of increasing wages, to all artisans who were anxious to advance.

Among men of ability are always men of heart. The lofty and wise activity of the prefect of the Seine, moved by the desire of the municipal council, which is the organ of art-interests, took the business in hand. A commission — presided over by the distinguished *savan* and friend of youth, M. Dumas, whom one finds at the head of all these generous organizations — was appointed. This commission obtained the firm and steady co-operation of the superintendent of the fine arts, and of the members of the institute, who formed a part of it. All have held it an honor to follow in minute details the execution of a plan which should have for the regeneration of art the most serious consequences. In a situation less elevated, but not less useful, we will mention the services of a young artist, M. Brongniart, secretary of the commission, and his colleague in the inspection of schools of drawing, M. Balze, both of whom have shown themselves patient and indefatigable, and who, in a few years, have given to all the schools uniform and excellent appointments, have organized the use of copies and models, and impressed everywhere habits of precision, of order, and a passion for duty.

"Many young persons, thanks to the labors of the commission and to the authority of the prefect, are now using, under excellent teachers, select copies and models, and attend courses of instruction which augment their zeal. Instruction in drawing has indeed revived in Paris. Even after we make allowance for the conditions, always more favorable in a large city, still we are compelled to say that the results far exceed what the rest of the empire can show. Charged simply with an examination, with a comparison perhaps, of different schools, doubtless it does not belong to us to advise such or such measures for establishing everywhere that equality of good which we have found at Paris. The resources and the obstacles must differ in each locality; but in recognizing a real superiority over the rest of France, or over foreign countries, we have desired to learn, as far as we could, the course pursued to produce such rapid improvement; and we believe the memorial of it ought to be preserved. This, briefly, is the substance of it: —

"Under the able magistracy of the prefect of the Seine, the universal desire for progress, at first manifested only by the municipal council, led that council to establish a commission, which should ascertain, beyond doubt, the exact state of instruction in drawing in the municipal schools. The commission devoted a year to investigations, as severe as important, in order to determine what reforms should be inaugurated, what capital they required; in a word, to determine by what means they could effect, in a durable manner, the reforms of which we have been able to state the marvellous results. These investigations once finished, the University hastened to give her co-operation to measures of which she could appreciate the full necessity. Funds were appropriated; and the realization of good did not linger.

"The examination made by the commission showed that there was in Paris a condition of things analogous to that which we find everywhere in France to-day, — that is to say, copies and models insufficient in number (generally of a very mediocre character, suggesting to the pupils a detestable past of commonplace), a small number of teachers, and, indeed, very inadequate appointments.

"This is what was done to obviate these various evils: in order to have better copies, after submitting to a severe purification all those in use, they appealed to the kindness of Count Nieuwerkerke, member of the commission, as well as superintendent of fine arts. Among the studies from nature which had gained medals for their authors during the course at the school of fine arts, he had search made for a certain number of figures hitherto overlooked, concealed at this school, and which now furnish the pupils of the municipal schools most precious resources. Then followed the happy thought of promising a recompense to the future laureates, when their figures should be taken as models for municipal instruction.

"For the same purpose, the pensioned pupils at Rome were required to send a certain number of drawings after the Italian masters, or after nature. Finally, M. Gérôme, member of the institute, colleague of Count Nieuwerkerke on the commission, undertook the task of having a limited quantity of lithographs made, which would serve to show the printsellers the new way it was resolved to try; to show them the impossibility of continuing to sell for the purposes of instruction, which was henceforth to be better, the productions of the past, which had been executed by contract, and without competition for honors. As to the teachers, the task was yet more difficult. This is how they satisfactorily met the difficulty: For many worthy artists it must be advantageous to give some hours to the instruction of youth, as a rest from other fatigues, other labors. This professorship, profitable alike to teacher and pupil, not only affords the teacher a money recompense, but it is an honorable title.

"Instead of choosing the teachers from among candidates with out guaranty, and upon information which might lead astray, they established competitive examinations and diplomas, which, elevating the level of studies by emulation, present the advantage of revealing the capacities and unknown aptitudes for imparting instruction. These diplomas, whose advantage had always been considered incontestable in other branches of education, produced a marvellous result. They afforded to Paris strong evidence of merit: they will afford, in the future, lists of capable teachers open to calls from the provinces and from abroad.

"Finally the commission (and this will be one of its titles to gratitude) made the competitive examinations established among the different pupils of its schools the object of a double recompense, — one for the students who were successful, and one for the teachers who had led to their success; the salaries of the teachers to be augmented according to the number of prizes obtained by the young laureates.

"We have, then, at Paris to-day, in the municipal schools, emulation of pupils and teachers, frequent examination of work, and certainty that they who teach carry not into their classes an indifference which might exist even with real talent. There is, thanks to this combination, the assurance of a union of efforts towards the same common end.

"As to the appointments, to speak the truth, and render justice to every one, I ought here to say, that they have been modified in the happiest manner, and do no less honor to the commission than to the zeal which their secretary displayed in changing completely the halls of drawing all along one bank of the Seine, and a portion of the other.

"All those who are occupied with education know how the love of labor is increased by objects apparently insignificant. One works better in a good class, where order reigns, under a good light. In looking at the magnificent appointments of Cluny, one of the examiners said to the director, that, if his hopes were to produce ordinary masters, the future would show chemists, *savans*, were it only for the magnificence of the laboratory, capable, in itself, of making all the youth dream of the institute.

"The good arrangements of the halls of drawing have contributed, we are convinced, to diffuse the taste and the habit of work among all the young draughtsmen in the suburbs of Paris; and we sincerely believe, that, if other cities were willing to imitate a movement which I have only been able to describe in a brief and incomplete manner, the results would be everywhere equally decisive.

"As to the special normal school at Cluny, I cannot do better than to quote here an extract from the report made by M. Dumas for the commission charged with the inspection of the establishment (June, 1867).

NORMAL SCHOOL OF CLUNY. — DRAWING.

"'The inspection of the instruction given at Cluny by the professor of drawing has been very satisfactory. The method, which is that of Hendricks, is as good as a method can be; for we must not expect to obtain decisive and heroic results, even from a very rational course of instruction, which can, at best, only develop the inborn tendencies, restrain dangerous impulses, and abridge the time of the studies.

"'The instruction at Cluny presents all these advantages. The professor is clear in his explanations, full of zeal; and one has only to approve what he has done. His pupils listen to him with attention, respect, and a desire to understand and to do well.

"'M. H. Dufresne, member of the Superior Council of Special Instruction, who has consented to accept the mission of judging the pupils of Cluny in relation to drawing, is at this moment charged as a juror, to examine, at the Universal Exposition, the different modes of instruction practised abroad. He has everywhere seen the Hendricks method produce good results. The geometrical tracings which form its basis permit one to compare exactly the proportions of the copy, facilitate enlargement or reduction, and habituate the pupil to discover for himself his errors, and to correct them. Leonardo da Vinci, and almost all the Italian masters, employed this method for their pupils and for themselves. Indeed, this mode of procedure is analogous to that of the sculptors for getting the proportions of their marbles, and gives the same results. This comparison is sufficient to indicate what are its advantages and its limitations.

"'It seems advisable, indeed, not to continue this manner of drawing for a long time, but to vary it sometimes; for example, by making the geometrical tracings after the execution of the figure, as a proof; or, perhaps, by confining them to certain points of division, to certain great lines of movement, so as to acquire the habit of drawing rapidly and with spirit, while drawing well.'

"Finally, I would conclude this report with certain practical hints as to the way in which we could wish that instruction in drawing should generally begin.

"'At the Universal Exposition,' says M. Cornu, my colleague, in a note which I produce entire, 'various methods of teaching drawing are exhibited by different nations, with the results obtained by each of them. These methods are rational. They are based, for mechanical drawing, on geometry. They are illustrated, for the most part, by figures in relief, and have mathematical exactitude. As to the methods of teaching drawing from copies, they depend upon principles and means of demonstration generally good and ingenious in their mode of application.

FORM, AND NOT SHADE, THE IMPORTANT THING FOR BEGINNERS.

"'The geometrical, machine, architectural drawings, &c., are more satisfactory, whatever be the nation to which they belong, than the copies of figures, flowers, and ornaments of the different classes of imitation-drawing. One might attribute this relative inferiority to the copies, defective in taste and form; also to a certain negligence in teaching. You cannot sufficiently combat the tendency of pupils to shade too much in order to arrive at effect, and to destroy their masses of light by too much detail, and their masses of shade by too much reflection. We cannot too often repeat, that the important point is, not to load a drawing with exaggerated lights and shades, which give an unnatural aspect to the object represented, but rather to render its true character by a faithful and intelligent outline, and by lights, shades, and half-tints in their proper place, and in relative and harmonious proportions.

"'Here are certain estimates of instruction in drawing abroad:—

ENGLAND.

"'The Kensington School presents at the Exposition an important collection of studies of different kinds. Some of these studies are very remarkable; notably, the flowers painted by Menzies, the ornaments in various styles, by Reule, Boon, and Collins, and also the drawings for paper-hangings by Chandler. It is evident that the pupils of this fine establishment have the best and rarest sources from which to draw. How, then, can we help being astonished at the difference which exists between the works which we have just named, and the figures painted in oil, in water-colors, or made with the crayon? Without speaking of a picture representing a woman bathing,—the execution of which, and the taste, leave much to be desired,—those studies are, in general, soft and affected, or in a hard manner, and jumbled in colors and effects. The drawings of anatomical figures, made with so much care and manual skill, as well as academical collections drawn too hastily, show clearly that it is more important and more difficult to give the true character of external forms and accuracy of movement than to give the minutest details of the muscles concealed under the skin.

AUSTRIA.

"'Many schools of drawing established at Vienna and in other cities of the empire have sent to the Exposition their methods of instruction and the works of their pupils. The school directed by Prof. Machatschek is one of the most important, and the one whose works are the most numerous and the most satisfactory. The section of architecture and mechanics, principally, offer a list of works executed with method, and in a laudable manner. It is to be regretted that the imitation-drawings of figures, of flowers, and of ornaments, as well as the model studies in bass-relief of divers styles, leave something to be desired in selection and execution. We make one exception for the Baugewerbe Schule of Vienna, whose drawings of ornament are in good taste, and well executed.

DENMARK.

"'The drawings by the pupils of the School of Copenhagen deserve to be honorably mentioned for the simple and intelligent manner in which they are done. One finds there, what is seldom seen in the works of pupils, the sobriety and harmony of effect, permitting form to predominate, making it serviceable, instead of destroying it, as so frequently happens. In conclusion, this exhibition does honor to the instruction and to the enlightened direction of the School of Copenhagen.

BAVARIA.

"'It is just to place in the first rank the Nuremberg School of Art and Industry. The beautiful exhibition of the products of its various departments do the greatest honor to its skilful direction, as well as to the talent and intelligent zeal of its professors. The drawing of figure and ornament, the modelling and sculpture, are explained and developed in a manner original and varied. From studies of heads, of draperies (whether in drawing or in relief), of portraits in historic costumes, of academic figures of small size to those which are drawn of natural size stumped on a shaded ground, there is a very remarkable specimen of the works of student painters and statuaries. The sculpture, more particularly decorative, shows, also, a very great quantity of ornamentation, composed almost wholly in the Gothic style, foliated and flowered a little beyond measure. In the whole number we discover but two or three bits in the Roman style. The Greek does not appear at all. This almost complete absence of the antique element must be attributed, without doubt, to the necessity of forming special sculptors to restore the ancient Gothic edifices injured by time, and also to ornament the new monuments erected in this same style so dear to Germans. Thus it happens that there is a void to be regretted in the instruction of the Nuremberg School. On the other hand, the course of study in the direction of invention and of composition of objects of industrial art appears excellent, and gives the best results.

WURTEMBERG.

"'A remarkable collection of plaster models, from elementary geometrical figures to the most complicated ornaments of pointed architecture, has been formed at Stuttgard by M. de Steinbeis. Mouldings of plants and foliage, most skilfully made from nature, supply the pupil with excellent subjects for study, and show him what assistance he can obtain from nature for decorative art. The judgment which presided over the creation of a course of drawing by mouldings after nature cannot approve the bad method followed in making the great black drawings which cover the walls of the Bavaria and Wurtemberg Exposition, — a method which consists in forcing the pupil to spend much time on complicated drawings, filled with heavy shades that are produced by great effort at hatching, and which teach them absolutely nothing.'

"Here are the theories of art, which we present to those who are delegated to teach. In other respects, the whole personal initiation is left to them."

HENRI DUFRESNE, *Reporter.*

PLAN OF TEACHING DRAWING AT THE ROYAL INDUSTRIAL SCHOOL IN NUREMBERG, ADOPTED IN NOVEMBER, 1869.

I. Ornamental drawing, preparatory class. (*a*) After ornamental models, twelve hours weekly. (*b*) Exercises in the drawing of surface ornaments, six hours weekly; Prof. F. C. Meyer.

II. Drawing from the antique, twenty-four hours weekly; Prof. Jaeger.

III. (*a*) Drawing from living models, groups of figures and drapery, twelve hours weekly; Supt. Kreling. (*b*) Drawing of heads, twelve hours weekly; Supt. Kreling and Prof. Jaeger. (*c*) Execution of cartoons, paintings on glass, &c.; Supt. Kreling and Prof. Wauderer.

Technical School. — First Course.

First Term (of six months). — Education of the eye and hand by the drawing of lines and geometrical figures. Full size drawing of bodies with plane surfaces. Explanation of the faculty of sight, and the first principles of perspective. Linear drawing without instruments is combined with free-hand drawing.

Second Term. — Continuation of free-hand drawing. Drawing of simple ornaments, from pictures fastened on the walls, or from slightly relieved or intersected objects. Linear drawing with the aid of square, and mathematical instruments. Division, measuring, and transfer of right lines, angles, and figures. Construction, gradation, and subdivision of scales.

Second Course.

Drawing of figures in relief. Drawing of compound ornaments, from "plastic" (*plastischen*) models. The proportion of the human head and its parts in firm, simple outlines, from pictures fastened on the walls. Exercises in the construction of regular curved lines. Architectural details. Projections of simple surfaces and plane circumscribed contours. Relief-drawing, after simple "plastic" objects in different proportions as to size.

Third Course.

Continuation of the exercises in free-hand drawing, curvilinear objects, drawing of animals and plants, — so far as applicable in ornaments, — with light shading to mark the form. Explanation of the manner of representing *style.* Drawing of the human body and its proportions in outlines. Linear drawing. Continuation of exercises in the drawing of projected figures, with reference to simple machines and models. The (five) orders of architecture. Industrial ornamentations and profiles, — if possible, in natural size, — after models. Sketching from nature. Exercises in India ink. Designs in intersection. Relief-drawing, after pictures of simple forms from the antique.

Agricultural School. — *First Course.*

First Term. — Training of the eye and hand in the drawing of lines, geometrical figures, and simple ornamental forms, from large pictures fastened on the walls. Drawing from correspondingly large bodies with plane surfaces. Explanation of the act of seeing, and the first elements of perspective.

Second Term. — Linear drawing, with the aid of square and instruments. Division into spaces. Measuring and transfer of straight lines, plane angles and figures. Construction and division of scales. Exercises in the drawing of simple geometrical bodies in outlines, and in various positions. The principles of projection.

Second Course.

Exercises in drawing of details of architecture, and especially arrangements of agricultural buildings, after models and original designs. Drawing of simple agricultural implements. Instruction in the designing of maps, and division of land into sections, intended for various agricultural purposes (*culturplänen*).

Third Course.

Exercises in the drawing of whole buildings, after models on a diminished or enlarged scale. Sketches of buildings in elevation and in profile. Drawing of agricultural implements and machines, after original designs.

Polytechnical School [*Real Gymnasium*]. — *First Course.*

Free-hand drawing. Exercises in the drawing of straight lines, and the formation of geometrical figures out of these lines. Drawing of bodies with plane surfaces, accompanied by explanations of the faculty of sight, and the first elements of perspective with reference to single figures and groups of figures. Exercises in the drawing of curved lines, and the formation of simple ornaments out of these lines. Drawing of symmetrical ornaments and implements, from pictures fastened on the walls, and from slightly-relieved plaster casts of antique forms of art.

Second Course.

Free-hand drawing. Division and relations of different parts of the human body, from pictures on the walls. Foreshortening of single parts in different positions; the form of the human body in different movements. Richer ornaments, round and plane, in outlines. Linear drawing. Exercises with rule, square, and compasses, by dottings or figures. Explanation of the principles of projection. Exercises in the delineation of simple bodies in projection. Measuring and reduction of models of bodies, and their projection according to various positions.

Third Course.

Free-hand drawing. Practice in the art of shading in its simplest form, — at first from plane-surface ornaments, afterwards from round. Heads in different positions; hands and feet, after easy models. Ornaments of different epochs of art, in connection with architectural details. Linear drawing. Measuring of compound models of bodies with plane surfaces, and their projection, by the application of geometrical rules, on an enlarged or reduced scale, according to position. Relief-drawing. Projection of ornamental details and of entire ornaments, — at first after solid, then after plane models, on an enlarged or diminished scale.

Fourth Course.

Free-hand drawing. Drawing of animals and plants, with close regard to foreshortening and oblique positions. Explanation of style, and its mode of presentation. Drawing of figures, after plane models. Ornamentation in conjunction with the human form, and forms of animals. Linear drawing. Projections of bodies with curvilinear surfaces, and their interjections. Drawing of the orders of architecture. Exercises in linear perspective, and shading of outlines. Construction of models. Execution of forms of crystals, and their transitions, in pasteboard, after original designs, in accordance with the rules of descriptive geometry.

With the authoritative testimony presented in this chapter, it cannot now be difficult to determine what should be the general scope and character of a course of drawing for common and special schools in this country, calculated to give both educational and industrial results of the highest order. Such a course of drawing, whatever may be said of details, must embody the leading features which are approved by the authorities here cited; as does, for instance, the course prepared by Prof. Walter Smith, Director of Art Education for the State of Massachusetts. For the purpose of preparing a course of instruction in drawing, and superintending its introduction into the public schools of the State, on the recommendation of the Science and Art Department of the British Government, Massachusetts and the city of Boston secured the services of Prof Smith, an English teacher of drawing and art, who had had an experience of many years as the head master of the school of art at Leeds, while he was familiar with the work done in the best Continental schools. With the results of European Art Education before us, and a clear understanding of our own needs, it does seem that there need be no more misconception of what is really meant by drawing, and no more serious blunders made in teaching it in this country.

CHAPTER VII.

CONCLUSION.

THE testimony of the preceding pages is conclusive, that, at this juncture in affairs, American labor should be thoroughly educated. It would be better for the laborer who is educated; since, by doing skilled work, his toil would bring him an ampler reward. It would be better for the employer; since, with the same capital, he would obtain products of greater value, while he would have, in the educated labor under his control, an assurance of stability, an assurance that others could not excel him, and drive him from his business. It would be better even for the laborer who is by nature so stupid that he cannot be educated; since the advancement of him who was educated to higher grades of employment would improve the chances, by diminishing the quantity, of ignorant bone and muscle. It would be better for the merchant; since it would enable him, in the markets of the world, to meet successfully the competition of the world with native products; and the markets of the world, to-day are no less the home than the foreign markets. It would be better for the State; since it would give her more intelligent, more thrifty, more virtuous citizens. Indeed, as educated labor is in every way the best, so in every way is it the cheapest labor in the world.

THE WORK MUST BEGIN IN THE PRIMARY SCHOOLS. — The testimony is also conclusive, that the education now required by the laborer must be much more than merely literary, much more than merely technical: it must be a due combination of both elements. The work, too, of imparting this education, must begin in the primary schools, — with language and mathematics, with art and natural science. In the higher public schools it must keep the same breadth, mainly leaving specialties of all kinds for special schools. There must be enlargement here, reduction there, all the way along the common-school curriculum, until we secure the popular education which the times demand for all, but especially for those who labor with their hands.

Consider what a large proportion of the pupils quit the public schools, never to enter them again, after they are thirteen years old. How essential, therefore, that some of the elements of a technical education should be taught in the primary schools! that pupils, before they are ten years old, should make a rational commencement with certain of the natural sciences and with drawing! It is always found, in attempting to acquire a knowledge of any new subject, that the most difficult part is to make a satisfactory beginning. Such beginning once made, farther progress becomes easy and rapid. That is one of the reasons why an adult of the average ability and spirit, but without any early technical education, so seldom attempts to make himself, by study, master of his business. If he is a farmer, for example, he cannot read the best books treating of agriculture, because he does not understand the chemical and botanical terms with which he meets, and without whose aid the books could not have been written. For the same reason, many of the best articles in his agricultural journal are for him a stumbling-block, and without profit. What is true ot the farmer is equally true of the carpenter, machinist, &c., if they have received no early technical instruction. It may be said they ought to set themselves studying the elements of those arts and sciences which bear upon their occupations, until they know enough to be able, at least, to read such books as would be of special service to them. But the great majority of them do not, and never will, if left entirely to themselves. Now and then, even in this country, we meet with men of considerable business capacity, men who have accumulated money, and yet cannot write their names. Rather than give the little time and labor which would be sufficient for learning to write their names, these men subject themselves to the continuous shame of making their mark. Though each needs to learn only the letters composing his own name, yet he goes on making a cross for his signature to the day of his death. This, indeed, is an extreme illustration of the inertia of the adult mind when the learning of something new is involved. But, for the writing of one's name, substitute the elements of any science or of drawing; then you have, for the average adult mind which has not been previously introduced to these mysteries, what will appear an overwhelming task. It may, indeed, be safely asserted, that, if all technical instruction is put off until the learner has become a workman, the instruction can never in any way, even with multiplied special schools, be made adequate to the requirements of the age. If, however, a proper beginning has been made in the common school, then there will be little difficulty with subsequent instruction.

But even if we could be assured that every child in the public schools would remain there until seventeen years old, and would afterwards attend suitable special schools, still it would be best to begin teaching the elements of natural science and art in the primary schools. Nearly every department of knowledge has features which are adapted to the minds of children, and which can often be better learned in childhood than at any later period. Notably this is true of drawing and of natural science. Both appeal to the perceptive faculties, and train the sight. Drawing deals with visible lines and forms: natural science deals with facts, phenomena, instead of words and abstract statements. Drawing cultivates the taste, confers manual dexterity, develops the inventive powers. The training which gives these things should begin early. Better than any other study adapted to childhood, natural science teaches to compare, to generalize, to tabulate, — things which pupils should begin to do at an early age, always providing that they are confined to things which they clearly comprehend.

CRAMMING. — Then you would devote the primary schools and public schools generally, it will be said, to the work of cramming pupils with a great and confused variety of facts, when they should quit the schools with a compact mass of knowledge, well arranged and well digested. Instead of giving them mental discipline, strong tendencies of mind to act in the right direction, you would leave them with good, strong habits of mind all unformed, the result of the vague impressions and fleeting influences to which they had been subjected by a too varied course of study. Certainly not. We would strive, and we believe successfully, for the just mean of knowledge and discipline, of formation and information; keeping two ends always in view, — the one educational, the other directly practical.

What is cramming? The mind must be supplied with a certain amount of facts, impressions, data, as the body must be supplied with a certain amount of food, before there can be digestion, assimilation, and growth. So long as the supply does not exceed the amount which can be well digested and assimilated, there is no cramming; and the young, growing mind, like the young, growing body, needs a large supply of food to keep it in healthy, prosperous condition. Just how much, it is, of course, impossible to tell. It is not necessary that the body be nourished with the same limited variety of food month after month, and year after year. Indeed, an occasional change is known to be decidedly advantageous. By the change, the relish with which the food is eaten is frequently increased, and, in consequence, the capacity for digestion and assimilation. Though there may be more eaten, as the result of the change, there is not, necessarily, any more cramming, — gluttony; because all that is eaten may be well used. A glutton may be gluttonous with a single dish. Change and variety of food do not, therefore, necessarily imply cramming for the body, but, rather, health and growth. Nor does variety in study necessarily imply cramming for the mind, but, rather, increase of knowledge and strength.

There may be just as much cramming with a few as with many studies. How often pupils in the public schools are compelled to learn the spelling of fifteen or twenty thousand words, and that, too, without heeding the laws of orthography, when there is no assurance that one pupil out of fifty will have occasion, in all his after-life, to write above three or four thousand different words, and those the most common! What is that but cramming? How often the pupils in the public schools are compelled to memorize, and that, too, with little reference to generalization, twenty to forty thousand facts in geography, when it is well known that not more than one-tenth part of these facts will be permanently remembered, or would be of any use if they were remembered! What is that but cramming? And what is that (which is sometimes done) but cramming, when children are made to memorize the solutions of numerous problems, and to learn a variety of arithmetical processes, yet are never required to compare one problem with another, nor one process with another, and never get a general view of arithmetical principles and their applications? And what is that but cramming, when children memorize whole grammars, and repeat them *verbatim*, while their discriminating powers are not equal to the comprehension of one-quarter of what they repeat? Yet if the pupils in the public schools are kept to spelling, arithmetic, geography, grammar, — the old recognized studies, — it is supposed by many that the evils of cramming will be avoided; while the truth of the matter is, that cramming in its worst form is usually found in those schools where the fewest studies are pursued, and where huge text-books receive their heartiest welcome. A large percentage of pupils now waste time enough in cramming with the spelling-book, to give them, if their energies were rightly directed, a rational, substantial start in botany. The common words which they will have occasion to spell after they leave school, they would spell as well as now; while their knowledge of botany, and the discipline derived from its study, would be so much clear gain.

Variety and Alternation of Studies. — With an increase in the number of studies, it by no means follows that they must all be pursued at once, but rather that they should be taken at intervals, with due alternation, as in the case of food. It is especially necessary in schools for the smaller children, that quite a variety of things should be taken in hand each day; since it is often impossible to keep the pupils, for any great length of time, interested in one thing, however well they may like it on the whole. When their interest is gone, there is no improvement; but, rather, disgust for school, for instruction, springs up. John Locke spoke very truly when he said a boy would soon tire of the sport, if he were required to spin his top a stated number of hours at the same time each day. And so it is with little children and their studies, however agreeable the studies may be in themselves. There must be a sufficient variety to give the children a healthy, unflagging interest in their work. Because there is not now such variety in many schools, the larger part of the time of the children is worse than wasted. The older the pupils are, and the better trained in applying themselves to study, the fewer the things which will suffice to give the requisite variety. If all the studies it is thought essential that pupils of a given age should be instructed in are not required for this purpose, then let the studies be taken at intervals; thus diminishing the number of lessons learned daily by the pupil, and the number of class-exercises conducted by the teacher.

The studies should not, however, alternate from day

to day, nor from week to week, but, rather, from month to month, or from term to term. It is, for several reasons, impossible to secure adequate results in any study, with a short lesson every third or every second day. Put the instruction which would thus be devoted to any study in three months all into one month, and very much more would be accomplished. Let the work, then, when any thing is done, be continuous and earnest.

There is no reason why arithmetic even, when once taken up, should be pursued without interruption until it is dropped finally. No harm, but, on the whole, good, rather, would come from dropping it; also geography and grammar an occasional term. The pupils would take up the work with renewed relish and vigor; what had been partially forgotten would soon be recovered; and then their advance over new ground would be more rapid than if there had been no period of rest. Experience justifies this declaration. If deemed advisable, however, that any general division of study should be pursued without any interruption, then, in the mathematics, for example, geometry might take the place of arithmetic, even with the youngest pupils. Natural science and drawing have, also, their different departments, which could be pursued with proper periods of alternation.

Room for Additional Studies. — Thus, if we reduce each study to its legitimate bounds, as determined by the two fundamental considerations, — the one educational, the other directly practical, — we can readily obtain place for additional studies in the public schools, and at the same time avoid the evils of cramming. While we give a pleasing variety to the studies in primary schools, utilizing all the time of the children with advantage to both their mental and physical health, we can at the same time, by giving to different studies intervals of rest, confine within a rational limit the number of lessons learned daily by the older pupils, and the number of class-exercises conducted daily by the teacher. Having done thus much, if we can then, without sacrificing any part of the economy of class instruction, so modify the present cast-iron system of graded public schools as to give the pupils in them an equal freedom with pupils in ungraded schools, enabling a large percentage of the pupils to accomplish in three years (and they are abundantly able to do it) what they are now compelled to spend five years upon, there will be yet more time gained for additional studies. This same change should also relieve the teachers of a part of their present responsibility for the advancement of their pupils, and put it where it belongs, — upon the pupils themselves, and upon their parents. The teacher would then become, what he should be, an assistant in the education of the pupil, or director at most. The self-reliance of the pupil and his love for his teacher, — who would be regarded as his friend, and not as his master, — would be greatly augmented. But if we cannot have these modifications in public-school instruction, then the new studies demanded by the times must go into the schools as they are, and each study take its chances. When parents and pupils see in schools certain new studies which have a direct bearing upon daily labor, the pupils will attend school a year or two longer for the sake of obtaining instruction that will tend directly to increase the returns for their toil. For the purpose of learning a little more geography, a little more arithmetic, a little more grammar, most pupils do not care to attend school, and most parents, we know, do not send them; but when there is seen in the schools something which will help them directly to become better farmers, better carpenters, better machinists, better artisans of every kind, the whole situation will be reversed, and a large part of the pupils who now leave school at such an early age will be found attending school a year or two longer if possible.

MENTAL DISCIPLINE. — What is discipline? To increase the number of studies will diminish, it may be said, the discipline which the mind should always derive from pursuing a course of study. Already it has been shown, that to enlarge the course of study will not, necessarily, enlarge the amount of cramming, — one of the worst features of bad instruction. But what of the variety? Though there should be no more cramming, will not the variety tend to give only vague, fleeting impressions, instead of strong tendencies in the right direction, instead of enduring habits of mind? Let us see. While each study has its peculiar characteristics both in matter and method, which exert a peculiar influence upon the mind of the learner, yet all studies have much in common; and the learner who has gained a knowledge of one finds it easier to gain a knowledge of all the others. The memory needs to be cultivated; but it should be cultivated in different directions. Pupils should not be kept constantly exercising their memory with one subject, — with the facts of geography alone, of arithmetic, of grammar, of science, of history. It is far better that it be exercised with various things, the pupil always shunning the fatal mistake of memorizing words according to the order of their sounds, and not of their meaning. Pupils should also learn to compare and discriminate; and this they can learn not only from the problems and processes of arithmetic, not only from the grammatical usage of words, not only from the phenomena of science and the forms of art, but best from them all combined. Pupils should learn to generalize and to tabulate; but no one study has a monopoly of these things. Pupils should learn application and self-reliance; but no study is without its obstacles and its demands for persistent effort. Hence it follows, that a change from one study to another does not break the continuity of the discipline: it only modifies the discipline, and, on the whole, for the better. Then there is a certain power and aptitude which comes from breadth of study, that can never be obtained from a narrow curriculum, and which enables one to do even special work better than the mere specialist. For this, among other reasons, no harm results when a study is occasionally discontinued for a brief interval, that another may be taken in its stead.

THOROUGH INSTRUCTION AND EXHAUSTIVE INSTRUCTION. — Great emphasis is justly laid upon thorough instruction; but the mistake is often made of putting *exhaustive* for *thorough*. One may know little of a given department of knowledge, yet know that little just as thoroughly as if he were acquainted with every thing that pertains to the department. One may have a clear comprehension of the great principles, laws, of any science, yet be totally ignorant of nine hundred and ninety-nine facts in every thousand known to be embraced by those principles or those laws. Now, it happens that too frequently text-books are made, and too frequently teachers attempt to teach, on the exhaustive plan. Cramming is the inevitable result, instead of rational instruction. Every text-book designed for public schools should be made, *first*, with reference to the best educational; *second*, with reference to the greatest practical, results derivable, not from one study, but from the whole course. Agreeably to these requirements, the books should be made large or small, more or less exhaustive, but always rational, always according to sound principles of instruction. And teachers of the public schools should always labor with the same objects in view, not unduly fostering one study, and neglecting another, because they chance to like the former, while they dislike the latter.

Text-Books in Natural Science. — The text-books of natural science which are designed for use in the public schools should attempt no more than a clear outline of each department, acquainting the pupils with only its leading and most characteristic facts, with its nomenclature, its general principles, and best methods of investigation. To do this, the books must be rationally constructed, having in view both an educational and a practical result. The different departments, — as botany, zoölogy, chemistry, mineralogy, — when they do not follow, can alternate with one another; that being taken which is best adapted to the season of the year.

Course of Drawing for Common Schools. — Since the testimony of the preceding pages is conclusive, that drawing should form the main feature in technical education designed for the great mass of the people, it will be well to add a few final words to what has already been said. The scope of the instruction, and, consequently, of the text-books, must be determined by the real needs of the people, and much or little be done accordingly. The needs, it is evident, are great; while the services which can be rendered by drawing are great also. Upon that we must proceed. The methods of instruction which are followed must aim to give both the best educational and the best practical results: they must be methods which have been justified by experience, or certainly methods which have not been condemned. Of course, original methods, unless they are absurd on their face, are never to be cavalierly dismissed.

A full and suitable course of drawing for public schools must include several clearly-defined departments. The whole must be systematically arranged, with reference, *first*, to logical order of principles; *second*, to difficulties of manual execution; *third*, to capacity of pupils at different ages; *fourth,* to sound principles of teaching. In a word, drawing is not a thing of vague uncertainties. It must be treated as should any other branch of study, that is, rationally, if it is expected to obtain satisfactory results. The two general divisions of drawing — free-hand and instrumental — may be divided into several minor departments, each having its peculiar characteristics. First, there should be free-hand drawing from copies in flat outline, dealing almost wholly with pure form. This work the youngest pupils should begin with slates, to be followed by similar but more elaborate drawings on paper. The practice in flat outline, while training the eye to distinguish beautiful forms, and the hand to draw them, should also teach, *first,* common geometrical figures; *second,* principles of practical design as applied to flat surfaces in woven fabrics and mural decoration, and to the contours of glass-ware, table-ware, and all kinds of pottery; *third,* some of the features which distinguish the art of different nations, as Egyptian, Greek, Roman, Gothic.

After a degree of skill in free-hand work has been acquired by the pupils, then should come mechanical drawing with instruments. This should concern itself mainly with those problems in plane geometry which are most extensively employed both in the construction of flat designs, and by carpenters, masons, machinists, and artisans generally. This instrumental drawing, since one of its educational objects is to teach the severest precision, should alternate, from day to day, with free-hand practice in flat-outline, which aims, among other things, to teach freedom of movement, and celerity of execution. This alternation has been found to help each kind of drawing: it tends to give accuracy in free-hand practice, and quickness in the manipulation of instruments.

Thus far, little or no thought has been given to the three dimensions, — to length, to breadth, and to height. Next in order, therefore, should come model and object drawing, which involves the three dimensions, and has for one of its educational aims the development of the imagination, that the pupil may be able to form a distinct mental picture of any object. This every one, but especially the artisan, has almost constant occasion to do. In this department, the leading subjects of study should be geometrical solids, manufactured objects specially illustrating geometrical forms, ornaments in relief, and natural objects having marked geometrical features, and illustrating principles of practical design. The models and objects, also the flat copies which should accompany them, should be beautiful as possible in form, that the taste may continue to be cultivated.

As but little can be done in this department without a knowledge of the principles of perspective, and as these principles cannot well be learned without drawing objects of three dimensions, it is quite proper that perspective drawing with instruments should alternate, from day to day or week to week, with free-hand drawing of models and objects. This work should begin in the grammar school, and conclude in the high school.

It is proper that the mechanical drawing of the figures of plane geometry should precede model and object drawing, and perspective. For how can one put a hexagon, for example, into perspective, unless he can first draw it geometrically? As perspective drawing, also model and object drawing, in the public schools, must be largely of the most practical nature possible, many of the objects drawn will necessarily have plane geometrical sides, contours. Unless, therefore, these objects can be drawn geometrically, that is, as they actually are, with their true proportions, it is impossible to draw them in perspective, that is, as they appear, with all their proportions modified by the laws of optics.

Before coming to object and model drawing, and to perspective, very little or nothing should be done with light and shade, and not very much then, though something. Form should predominate. There remains one other, a fifth, general department of drawing which can imperatively claim a place in the public schools; and that is mechanical projection. This should be so far taught as to give the principles which are common to all kinds of construction, — architecture, machinery, bridge-building, and the like. The object should not be to make draughtsmen, — a work properly belonging to special schools, — but to enable the pupils readily to read working-drawings. Whether this department of instrumental drawing be taken before perspective among the less advanced pupils, or after perspective among the more advanced pupils, it should be, in the main or wholly, an elective study, to be pursued by those who will probably engage in some kind of building construction.

This is a general outline of what must constitute a practical and artistic course of drawing for the public schools. It is certainly the least that should be taken. While the general features must be such as have been described, there may, of course, be minor modifications to meet the requirements of local circumstances. For the more advanced pupils, especially for those showing a marked aptitude for art, there should be added, in the high school, more drawing from nature and from the cast, with greater attention given to light and shade.

For each department of drawing, even for model and object, there should be text-books. They should be few or many, large or small, according to the requirements of the work to be done. They should contain drawings to be executed, directions for executing them, and full, clear explanation of the principles involved, that the pupils may become much more than mere copyists. Such a text, lessening the labor of the teacher, and generally diffusing the principles of art, has a value hardly second to that of the drawing-copies themselves, though the latter are, what they always should be, beautiful in design, and perfectly accurate in drawing. With such books in the hands of the pupils, it is far from a necessity that the teacher should be an expert in manual execution. Indeed, the regular teachers of the public schools, possessing the great advantage of a general knowledge of teaching, can always do excellent work, aided by such books as have been described. They will usually excel the mere draughtsman in the schoolroom. But if the teachers of the public schools were all expert at drawing, even then the pupils should be supplied with such text-books as have been described, and not be left to receive their instruction wholly from the teachers, who would thus find their labors greatly increased, while the advancement made by the pupils would be much less rapid. It should be one of the chief aims of the public school to teach the pupils how to use a book properly. Only a small part of them now learn this lesson, upon which depends so much of their progress in knowledge after leaving school. They learn to memorize the words of the text-books; but the real meaning of the words, that, too frequently, they fail to learn. Now, aside from diminishing the labor of the teacher, and accelerating the advancement of the pupil, the execution of a drawing, especially an instrumental drawing, from a printed text, is one of the best possible exercises for teaching a pupil the exact force of words. If he follows minutely the directions of the text, he obtains a correct result: if he mistakes the meaning of the words, his drawing is wrong, and he needs no one to tell him it is wrong. He has only to begin again, studying his text with greater care. It is not a matter of memorizing words, as it might be in almost any other study; but he must ascertain just what the words mean, and then do just what that meaning requires. This is a decidedly important educational feature.

A large part of the drawing copies and models, especially in the early stages of instruction, should possess definite general proportions, and strongly-marked geometrical features, which can be indicated by construction-lines or geometrical tracings. To make use of these helping lines is to follow the practice of the best masters of different ages. By their aid the pupil does his work understandingly: he is enabled to make his drawings larger or smaller than the copies, — an essential matter. It is the true way to approach the study of Nature; for Nature, in her general features, usually builds upon regular geometrical forms, however much she may deviate from them in details. Unless the pupil can first draw that which is regular, symmetrical, of definite proportions, and which can therefore always be verified, how is it possible for him to draw an object, whether of nature or art, which is irregular, unsymmetrical (if only in details), which has no definite proportions, and so does not permit the drawing to be verified by measurement?

The blackboard should be frequently used by the teacher for the purpose of class-instruction in principles and in the execution of drawings. Time is thus saved. It should also be quite frequently used for the purpose of supplying the pupils with copies to draw to a much smaller scale on paper. They thus learn reduction. The pupils themselves should often draw on the blackboard, enlarging the copies in their books. Thus they learn enlargement, while they acquire great freedom and boldness of movement.

Pupils should frequently make drawings, the features being orally dictated by the teacher, instead of always drawing from copies, models, objects. This will test their knowledge of what they have been over; will show them that words and lines, forms, are convertible, while it will develop the imagination: since it will be impossible for them to draw a single line correctly, unless a mental picture of it has first been made. If we consider the practical view alone, it is exceedingly important that the imagination should thus be trained; for every one must at times work under oral orders. Pupils should also be exercised in the reproduction from memory of drawings previously executed; especially should they be thus exercised in drawing noted historic forms, until the distinguishing peculiarities of these forms are indelibly traced upon the memory. In this way, not only will the memory be strengthened, but the pupils will acquire the power of distinguishing the features which characterize the art of different nations and of different ages. But especially should pupils be exercised in that most delightful and most profitable kind of drawing, — original design. Having learned some of the principles which should both direct and restrain the invention, and having become acquainted with some of the historic materials to be used, also with the method of procuring new materials from the exhaustless sources of Nature, there can be no end to the delight, to the intellectual stimulus, to be obtained from the practice of original design.

Special Instruction. — A broad, rational foundation for art and science to build upon having first been laid in the common schools, special schools of all grades, for students and for workmen, and museums, should be at once established throughout the country. What should be the general character of these special schools and museums has been clearly outlined in the preceding pages. It is not proposed, here and at this time, to give details, but simply to urge that such schools and museums be established at the earliest day, upon the broadest, most liberal foundation, and at all those central points where their influence upon the local industries will be the most direct, the soonest felt and recognized. While the technical instruction given in the common schools will tend to swell largely the numbers found in the higher special schools, the influence of the latter will also tend greatly to elevate the technical instruction of the former, just as the higher classical instruction of the academies and colleges has, in the past, tended greatly to elevate the literary instruction of the common schools.

INDEX.

E.

F.

K.

L.

M.

www.ingramcontent.com/pod-product-compliance
Lightning Source LLC
La Vergne TN
LVHW010220110826
845151LV00004B/1159

* 9 7 8 1 4 2 5 5 2 6 1 1 5 *